Just a Bite

A Transylvania Vampire Expert's
Short History of the Undead

ISTVÁN PIVÁRCSI

New Europe Books

Published by New Europe Books, 2012
Williamstown, Massachusetts
www.NewEuropeBooks.com

Library of Congress Cataloging-in-Publication Data
Pivárcsi, István.
Just a Bite: A Transylvania Vampire Expert's Short History of the
Undead / István Pivárcsi; [translation by Dorottya Olchváry, Dániel
Dányi, and Paul Olchváry]. —1st ed.
p. cm.
Includes bibliographical references and index.
ISBN 978-0-9825781-4-8 (alk. paper)
1. Vampires. 2. Dracula, Count (Fictitious character) 3. Monsters. 4.
Torture. I. Title.
GR830.V3P63 2012
398.21—dc23
2012008356

1 3 5 7 9 10 8 6 4 2

TABLE OF CONTENTS

Preface

Just a Bite

A Transylvania Vampire Expert's
Short History of the Undead

ISTVÁN PIVÁRCSI

 New Europe Books

Preface

If there is one thing that is truly and quintessentially human, it is the world of fantasy. Since childhood I've been keenly aware that I imagine things all the time, and given that this happens every bit as much to most other people and that we share such musings with others, it is not hard to appreciate how what we might collectively term "mythology" or "the universe of the collective imagination" developed out of all this. At the same time there is a bit of conscious human chicanery at work in imagining our imaginations to be so unique a trait, is there not? After all, we have yet to rule out the possibility that snails, for example, have active imaginations of some sort, and if they do, whether they too share their musings with each other.

In studying to become a historian, I was taught to believe only in facts and to be as honorable as possible in drawing conclusions from them. And yet I quickly realized that when considering a historical event, it wasn't so much the *when* and the *why* that interested me, but rather, what those persons who had participated in the given event were *thinking* when all this happened to them and/or on account of them. This led me to a love of two integrally related disciplines—folklore and cultural history—that, while today firmly established in universities across the world, are still taken less than seriously by all too many people.

From there came my interest in, and research into, vampires. Add to this the fact that practically the whole mythology of vampires emerged in the very Eastern Europe where I was born and raised and live to this day as a native speaker of Hungarian. This, coupled with my academic interests, meant a unique opportunity for me to thus deepen my knowledge by way of first-hand research in Transylvania—which, though part of Romania since the early twentieth century, is still home to some two million ethnic Hungarians, who can also be found in other nearby regions of particular relevance to vampires, including the Balkans and parts of Ukraine. *Just a Bite* consequently draws as much on the works of Hungarian folklorists and others have who conducted research across such territories from the early twentieth century on—authorities whose works you will find in the bibliography—as it does on my disparate experiences in the field.

At the end of the nineteenth century, vampire mythology made a decisive break from the minds of those who lived in the villages of Transylvania and neighboring regions and broadened its horizons first to literature, then film, and later it became a favorite theme of other areas of the arts. What stirs me most is how it left its origins, the world of popular folk mythology, behind, as it were, and acquired a life of its own in the imagination of so many artists. This question is vital also because, of course, vampire stories are alive and well to this day in the arts—and in particular on the silver screen—becoming all the richer as they acquire newer and newer content.

That being said, *Just a Bite* is focused unabashedly more on the historical than on so many contemporary vampiric "sound bites" all over the tube, the silver screen, the virtual world, and our collective imagination these days. The Transylvania I know and love from decades of study and travel, and that the world knows—or doesn't really know?—as the birthplace of Count Dracula, is in some respects still a world apart; a world steeped in the rich fabric of human history and folklore that gave birth to so much of what lies just behind the surface of so many newfangled fanged fables.

The two questions most frequently posed to me by my students are these: Are there vampires? Do I believe in vampires? My answers to both are simple and more or less the same. As a teacher, I seek above all to clarify what it is that we should be in the business of calling "real." Having made clear the centrality of this pursuit, I then try focusing attention on the fact that *everything* that exists in nature and in the human mind is part of reality. In short, then: vampires undoubtedly do exist, even if this is the case only in our imaginations and, consequently, as part and parcel of our cultural heritage as well.

Finally, a word on my narrative approach. This book represents one Hungarian historian and traveler's sometimes elusive but ever conscientious filtering of numerous sources—sources including not only those books listed in the bibliography (some folkloric works available only in Hungarian) but also Hungarian-language and other archival materials and, indeed, stories heard during many journeys over many years in Transylvania and elsewhere in the region. As it is intended not so much as a scholarly work but more an information-rich, readable reference that provides a broad glimpse into our enduring and yet ever-evolving fascination with the undead, rather than providing citations throughout I opted to write it more or less as the information came to me—and, as perhaps befits a scholar, removing myself from the scene, as it were, in the third person.

Hence, what you do in fact get is a Transylvania vampire expert's necessarily subjective and, I trust, authoritative broad view of the subject. I would then kindly ask those readers inclined to further, in-depth study of the undead to head to the library and seek out works well endowed with footnotes or endnotes or with many more pages to plod through; indeed, I'd encourage them to do so. Thank you for bearing with me, and please don't worry if you feel something tickling your neck in the middle of the night if you've fallen asleep with this book by your side. It's just your imagination. Or is it just a bite?

István Pivárcsi, Budapest, 2012

Part I
The World of Blood

Chapter 1

Vampirology

Dear Reader: Welcome to my castle. Excuse us if it is a little crowded, but we live in a world obsessed with vampires. Never have so many people turned to our sinister undead friend for chills; never before have there been so many vampire sleuths, vampire tourists, and even vampire wannabes. But have some patience, have some sympathy, and here you will come to see the historical and cultural roots of our modern-day fascination with vampires. It will be a long night, filled with real and imagined places, blood libel and gory executions, and—of course— Dracula himself will make an appearance. Fictional characters aside, you may even meet a real-life vampire or two.

You do believe in vampires, don't you?

Most anything, real or not, can be studied in one way or another, and vampires are no exception. But just what is "vampirology"—if we may use this lofty

term—all about? Well, it might be seen on the one hand as a peculiar niche of knowledge whose students examine the development and dissemination of vampire mythology, not to mention the historical and cultural facets of this mythology. Thorough research is of course required to undertake such study in a manner that would pass muster with a PhD committee; this in turn presumes that you can navigate your way comfortably about such relevant disciplines as history, ethnology, literary history, and even biology and medicine. Whether vampirology will ever quite become a subfield of humanities in its own right seems in question, though a cursory online search does turn up vast numbers of people who don't let this stop them. This leads us to another sort of vampirology—one whose practitioners, while likewise intrigued by cultural phenomena, do not much bother with what a PhD committee would say. This approach presumes either a belief in the existence of vampires or an all-encompassing fascination almost akin to belief—a state of mind in which mythology mobilizes the imagination while satisfying one's need for bloodcurdling thrills.

So where did vampires come from? What sort of sinister beings did we humans imagine in the centuries before we dreamed up the vampires we know and love today?

As understood by those European folk traditions linked most closely with the evolution of today's world-famous, fanged creatures of the night, vampires belonged partly to this world and partly to the next—"transitional" beings, as they were called in medieval times. And, yes, they fed on human blood. But cast aside that cherished image of Count Dracula! Vampires in fact appeared in the Old World imagination early on more as bestial, animallike monsters rather than in human form. Similar creatures sharing human and animal traits had already

populated ancient Mesopotamian, Egyptian, Phoe-
nician, Greek, and Roman myths. The Greek world,
for example, was home to Delphyne, a dragon whose
body was half-snake and half-woman; Hydra, the
hundred-headed monster of the Lernean swamps;
and the man-eating, bullheaded, man-bodied Minotaur.

In the medieval European world of Chris-
tianity-steeped folklore, monsters comprised three
broad categories, based on their physical nature and
their ability to assume various forms:

• Disembodied creatures from the afterlife
• Embodied creatures from the afterlife—
which is to say, those capable of assuming bodily
form on entering this world
• Human beings in this world who had
morphed into monsters

Such classification led, long last, by the
seventeenth and eighteenth centuries, to that all-
important step: the ascribing of human form to
vampires. At the same time, these "human" vampires,
in line with more ancient beliefs, were still capable
of extraordinary transmutation into various animal
forms as well—most notably, as bats or wolves.

Let us now turn our attention briefly to three
broad realms of cultural practice prevalent among

humans since ancient times that, over the years, came together in the form of vampire legends.

RETURNING FROM THE GRAVE

It seems appropriate to begin with that which consumes the attention of humankind more than anything else, alongside life, taxes, and sex: *death*. More specifically, the worship of the dead and, in particular, the conviction prevalent in primitive times and common throughout parts of Europe into the Middle Ages and beyond that the dead were capable of rising from their graves to visit their loved ones; or, say, of wreaking revenge on their former oppressors and sundry wrongdoers.

Since death was typically seen as a separation of body and soul, a return from the grave was necessarily imagined as a return in spiritual rather than physical form, and thus arose legends of ghosts, demons, and other such nasty apparitions. In fact, only in relatively recent times did the concept of the *body itself* returning from the realm of the dead to haunt the living gain currency. As for vampires, as early legends made clear, they included hapless humans who could not quite bring themselves to kick the bucket; more precisely, their souls did not wholly separate from their bodies at what for all intents and purposes appeared to be their dying breath. Thus, on returning from the beyond, they haunted the living in both body *and* spirit.

BLOOD, THE LIQUID OF LIFE

As even amateur vampirologists know full well, vampires can survive only by ravenously sucking blood, thereby securing the nourishment they need. Thus we arrive at another realm of relevant folklore: the mythology of blood. One of the most ancient themes of all, preoccupation with blood in folklore stems from the conviction developed in the human mind in prehistoric times that blood is both a—or *the*—prime source and sustainer of life. It was a common belief among many tribal societies that by taking the blood or the lives of others—not least, of their foes—those who managed to do so would live longer. In some ancient cultures, daubing the skin with an enemy's blood was held to bring magical power. So too, human and blood sacrifices came to be performed for the gods, and blood pacts sealed communal contracts. And, indeed, legends arose featuring bloodsucking animals that transform into demonic beings capable of leeching a person's life force by sucking his or her blood. Alongside its awareness of real-life bloodsucking pests such as lice and ticks, the human mind has given rise to myths of bloodsucking bats and werewolves that not only extract blood from their victims, but also kill them. As these legends evolved, bloodsucking animals mutated into horrible monsters, and then—the legends having commingled with the worship of the dead—the creatures assumed human form and became full-fledged transitional beings.

DARKNESS AND DOOM

The concept of darkness has likewise been bound up with vampire legends from the start. Since ancient times, human beings have been terrified of the unknown and its visual manifestation, night, feeling vulnerable in its presence. The ancient Greeks and Romans tended to draw a sharp distinction between light and dark, considering the former a source of life and thus a symbol of fertility and life on Earth, while darkness represented the forces of evil and destruction—in a nutshell, death and the afterlife.

Nor did this link between darkness and doom wane in the centuries to come. In Christian Europe of the Middle Ages, darkness was seen, not surprisingly, as the dominion of Satan. Demons, evil spirits, and witches were presumed to prefer nighttime to wreak their wicked deeds and supernatural havoc.

Such thinking thus lent a special significance to beliefs associated with midnight and the full moon. Demonic forces traditionally go on the prowl beginning at midnight. This is the witching hour, when human beings capable of transforming into bloodthirsty wild animals become active—and when bloodsucking vampires rise from their graves to go off in search of victims.

POWER AND POSSESSION

These three paramount mythological roots of vampire legends—the worship of the dead, the mythology of blood, and the concept of darkness—took on ever more associations as the centuries passed. Among them was one that later became decisive as regards the theme at issue here: the view that the vampire, wielding a demonic force, acquires supernatural power over its victims, putting them in service of its sordid ends; and, at its convenience, finally annihilating them.

It was not physical strength that allowed vampires to do all this, that is, but their otherworldly, spiritual superiority. Recent centuries saw erotic, sexual overtones come into play as well, yielding the belief that the vampire drains the will of its weak, feminine victim, whereupon it—or, rather, he—possesses her in the most complete way imaginable.

The roots of this notion reach far back. The ancient Chaldeans, who ruled over Babylon around the sixth century bc, held that sucking blood was a singular manifestation of sexuality. The Romans saw the lamiai, or evil sylphs, that populated their mythology as not only demonically powerful harlots but also bloodsuckers. However, this erotic motif really came to the fore in vampire legends during the Romantic era of the nineteenth century.

FROM THE SLAVS TO THE HUNGARIANS
TO TRANSYLVANIA

While unequivocally determining just when and in what circumstances vampires—or, more precisely, accounts and legends concerning them—first arose is a tall order, their origins seem to go back to the eastern Slavic peoples in the Balkans at some point during the Middle Ages. The earliest known written records concerning the existence of vampires can be traced to this general location and time period, at any rate; and indeed, some such records bear the signatures of numerous witnesses.

Although research has found that vampire myths are rooted most firmly in Serbian, Croatian, Ukrainian, Romanian, and Ruthenian folklore, the mythology of vampires nonetheless became inter-twined, above all, with the onetime Kingdom of Hungary—and, within its sweeping dominion, the largely mountainous and mysterious region of Tran-sylvania. Hungary, in a national trauma whose rever-berations stir many a Magyar soul to this day, was forced to relinquish this territory to Romania under the Treaty of Trianon in 1920.

　　Why Transylvania? Largely because the vam-pire that was to become best known by name, Count Dracula, was linked in the popular imagination to that region—despite the fact that Vlad Țepeș (of the House of Drăculești—i.e., Dracula), the actual per-son Dracula was based upon, was a Romanian who ruled not in Transylvania at all, but in Wallachia, which comprises much of the southern portion of modern-day Romania; that is, *south* of Transylvania.

　　Romanian folklore in particular came to be permeated by vampires, thanks in no small part to a certain tenet of the Eastern Orthodox Church—namely, that those people who died after being excommunicated returned as the walking dead—*moroi* in Romanian. Indeed, such souls were con-demned to remain in this most unfortunate state of limbo until the Church saw fit to relieve them of the curse. Another ancient demonic creature inhab-iting Romanian folklore was the *strigoi*: a nocturnal death-bird with supernatural powers that flew about

Vampire on a building façade in Waidhofen, Austria. Photo © M. Henderson Ellis

at night, hunting human flesh and blood. Etymologically speaking, this weird and winged creature can be traced back to the term *striga*, used through much of Europe during the Middle Ages to denote a certain kind of witch.

It was, in short, the merging of those traits ascribed to *moroi* and *strioi* that yielded the characteristic Romanian vampire figure whose modern permutations we have come to know. Linked as they were to the Christian religious tradition that pervaded nearly every aspect of society, vampires became seen as agents of Satan, as instruments of

evil bent on violating and annihilating humanity—
and it was thought that a whole army of them were
out there in the night maneuvering for final victory.
They fed on human blood, and their bite infected
their victims with vampirism. Blood and darkness
alone sustained them.

Sound familiar? That's because this is essentially the iconic figure that stirs the minds of practically all students of vampirology to this day. Though
technically immortal, the vampire is certainly not
invulnerable. But its physical manifestation can be
destroyed only with special abilities and tools. Do
you think we would initiate you into this dark realm
without giving you defenses? Read on.

Chapter 2

Fending Off Vampires

Those who believe in the existence of vampires—whether in momentary flights of fancy or as part and parcel of a more sustained frame of mind—have long been concerned with how to keep these pernicious creatures away; or, should doing so prove impossible, how to fend off attacking vampires and destroy them. One of the basic premises of vampire lore is the notion that vampires, despite being immortal, are liable to injury. Of course, to injure or destroy a vampire you must be able to recognize it; and this requires familiarity with the *vampiric nature*.

HEAVY ON THE GARLIC, PLEASE

It doesn't take a deep knowledge of Romanian folklore to know that vampires fear garlic, but some such knowledge can't hurt should the beast appear at your window (feel free to pause here and close the shades). Indeed, the consumption of garlic, as well as the placing of garlic wreaths at various points of a house, were regarded for many vampire-minded generations across Romania as among the most effective means of protection. In some areas, hapless folks who had an unadventurous palate and didn't care for garlic fell under suspicion of being vampires.

How to spice up your life while warding off the vampire menace? By rubbing all doors and windows with garlic, of course. If we consider that most humble village homes had just two rooms—a kitchen and a bedroom—it is not hard to imagine that the odors of garlic, moldy-musty tamped-earth flooring, cooking-lard, and wood smoke yielded a reek that permeated furniture, utensils, clothing . . . and people.

Garlic has long been regarded as a source of vitality and health by cultures far afield, and was treasured even in Antiquity. The Babylonians, Greeks, and Romans are the most prominent among those ancient peoples that used garlic as a remedy. Medieval herb books all classified it as among the most virtuous of plants, abounding in energy and vigor. Treasured as a universal cure-all, garlic was used to treat a wide range of ailments, to prevent illnesses, and indeed, to counter hexes.

Garlic originated in Asia, and went on to become the primary garden herb across much of

Eastern Europe—a core ingredient in Slavic, Hungarian, and Romanian cuisine for centuries. It was believed to be so distressing to vampires precisely because they were presumed to be incapable of defying the potent *life* force evident in its overpowering smell and flavor—as modern science has since determined, the compound allicin, an amino acid found in its oil.

In some legends, vampires are simply unable to suck the garlic-fortified blood of their prospective victims; and even if they do succeed, they are unable to draw from it the sort of life-giving nourishment that they, vampires, need. It is fair to say that garlic does not agree with their palate.

WEAR YOUR CHRISTIANITY ON YOUR SLEEVE, OR AROUND YOUR NECK

In the Christian faith, demonic beings were held to be in league with Satan, and vampires were right up there with the most evil. As physical manifestations of Satan, they naturally had to stay on guard against all sacraments of the Church. Hence legends abound in which vampires recoiled in horror on being confronted by the sign of the cross, crucifixes, and amulets, and were known also to beat a hasty retreat at the mere mention of Jesus or the Virgin

Mary. In his 1897 novel *Dracula*, Bram Stoker frequently alludes to such beliefs. For example, when the protagonist, English solicitor Jonathan Harker, takes a rest along his journey to visit Count Dracula, he encounters local peasants who, after learning of his mission, repeatedly utter the words "Satan" and "hell" in Hungarian, Slovak, and Serbian and point at him while making the sign of the Cross. In a later scene, when Harker is a guest of the Count, he accidentally cuts himself while shaving. Unable to resist the sight of blood, the Count reaches for Harker's throat, but in doing do he accidentally touches the cross hanging from Harker's neck. Count Dracula recoils in terror.

In Christian-influenced vampire lore, vampirism was seen as a unique manifestation of either damnation or penitence: Those who passed their

lives wallowing in despicable sin faced damnation in the afterlife. In short, there was no rest for the wicked, not even in their graves. Alas, after rising from the grave, it became their mission to acquire yet more victims for their lord, Satan, who possessed their souls.

CREATURES OF THE NIGHT

What better way, then, of countering a vampire's satanic ends than with the pure self-sacrifice of an innocent, most delicate woman? Easier said than done: the vampire must be in her presence at daybreak (read: at the first cock-crow). Still, the news is heartening: not only can good vanquish evil, but so too can daylight.

Doomed to eternal darkness, vampires are deathly pale, with waxy complexions. In Stoker's novel, Harker finds himself locked in the Count's rundown old castle, whose high Gothic windows don't let in even a single beam of sunlight. Dwelling alone in the bleak, cryptically dark building, Dracula, lord of the castle, appears before his guest only at night.

No need to fear vampires by the light of day, then, for they take care to retreat to their crypts and coffins before dawn, whereupon they pass the day in hiding and repose. No sooner does the sun go down, though, that vampires turn active once more, their dark powers recharged for their nightly round of hunting.

In centuries past, this did not bode well for insomniacs in many a Romanian village, who were sometimes accused by their fellow neighbors of vampirism. Individuals under such suspicion would on occasion be put to the test; for example, by being made to stand swelteringly close to a huge bonfire that would illuminate their entire figures, or else by having lamps or candles held within inches of their faces. Could they take the heat? Candlelight eventually came to be seen as too ineffectual to deal vampires any damage, however. Hence nine-teenth-century stories often see vampires willingly appear before their victims by candlelight, which, by enhancing their own human traits, allows them-selves to avoid detection.

VAMPIRE HUNTERS AND
THEIR CUTTING-EDGE METHODS

Not surprisingly, the most prominent and heroic figure in vampire tales of the Romantic era became *the vampire hunter*. Usually a scientist, he was invari-ably well versed in arcane rituals and the occult, pos-sessing an in-depth knowledge of vampires' hiding habits and other salient traits. Thus he had a con-siderable advantage over the average person when it came to both recognizing vampires and, of course, destroying them. That is not to say folklore isn't rife with vampire-destroying methods that in fact carried over into real life: terrified villagers often disposed of bats they found holed up in attics by driving sharp wooden stakes through their tiny hearts, convinced that they were also keeping potential vampires at bay.

According to one medieval account, a suspicious corpse unearthed months after its interment was found to have a completely preserved body. To be on the safe side, a wooden stake was driven through its heart, whereupon fresh blood gushed up—proof positive that it was a vampire. Although this particular vampire had already been successfully terminated with the wooden stake, it was then cremated as well, just in case.

Granted, it is highly unlikely that impalement as a much-favored method of execution in Eastern European during the Middle Ages was conceived as a precaution against vampires. But the parallel is striking.

Yet another written record of a suspected vampire's exhumation from times gone by notes that the corpse was decapitated—so as to render the bodiless head incapable of movement and, of course, the headless body incapable of sucking blood.

Indeed, assuming they didn't meet their end that way to begin with, ill-stared individuals suspected of being vampires could expect to be decapitated soon after they died, and to have their severed heads buried somewhere far from the rest of their mortal remains.

"Le Vampire," engraving by R. de Moraine. From his book Les tribunaux secrets, 1864.

Chapter 3

Bloodsucking Bats

In some corners of the world far removed from Eastern Europe, one starting point for the creation of vampire legends was the fact that some species of animals feed by sucking the blood of other living creatures. While no one has ever seen the need to drive a stake through the heart of a mosquito, in South America there are larger animals, so-called vampire bats, that specialize in sucking blood using their razor-sharp front teeth. Bats are the world's only mammals capable of sustained flight. On their upper extremities all the fingers but the first are successively longer, and connected by a membrane of skin that also links their sides, their legs, and their tail—a membrane that makes for rather awkward going on the ground. Vampires made to order, bats are nocturnal, spending most of the day hanging upside down in tree hollows, caves; or, closer to home, attics. All their teeth are equipped with needlelike points. While their eyesight leaves much to be desired, they ably find their way about in the dark by emitting sonar that bounces off objects and alerts them to edible insects.

What with their nocturnal habits; their mouselike bodies; their dark, intricately cut wings; their unsettling, ratlike faces; and their weird, high-pitched screeches—bats, it seems, were fated by Mother Nature to be regarded by most of humanity as hideous, frightful creatures. It should come as no surprise, then, that in medieval Europe, angels and good spirits were commonly depicted in art as rising up high on feathered wings, while devils and demons were left to flap around on bat wings. Monsters and dragons were likewise portrayed with membranous wings. Surely such paintings stirred the superstition-rich souls of medieval people, and not in such a way as to counter negative biases about bats.

FLYING FOXES

Notwithstanding the effect upon the human psyche of bats' appearance and nocturnal ways, in Europe and most other reaches of the world, at least, their eating habits didn't play a role in the association that was to be drawn over the centuries between them and those satanic, transitional beings known as vampires. All Old World bat species feed on insects,

Vampire bat (vintage illustration from Meyers Konversations-Lexik on 1897)

and many in Asia are partial to fruit—including the world's largest bats, those species in the genus commonly called "flying foxes." Only a few South American bats are able to suck blood—using a specially differentiated tongue, and only in the event that they cannot secure other nutrition. The sixteenth-century Swiss naturalist Conrad Gesner (1516–1565) sought to get to the bottom of folk tales concerning bloodsucking bats, relying on the eyewitness testimonies of missionaries who had settled in South America. In one of his accounts he wrote:

> In . . . the New World, the Spanish were tortured by bats. Those bitten as they sleep died of blood loss. If such bats come across a hen or a rooster, they grab its comb with their claws and kill it. In some regions . . . the Spanish saw bats not smaller than a dove, and when they tried to shoot them

during the night, they got covered by their poisonous bites, and it was all they could do to run away. Similar bats live on the island of Cuba. . . . In the experience of some, these are every bit as dangerous . . . Others say that their bites . . . heal immediately when washed with seawater.

In contrast with Gesner's observations, today we can say definitively that no bloodsucking bat is able to kill a large animal, and that even the most egregious examples of such species' behavior has them generally content with tapping their victim's blood, as it were, more or less harmlessly, rather than biting and/or sucking their prey to death.

THE WHOLE TRUTH ABOUT VAMPIRE BATS

Here is another fact ripe for party conversation while holding that Bloody Mary: while admittedly no beauty, that particular South America species that first became known as the "vampire bat" rarely exceeds seven inches in wingspan—and, more to the point, it is harmless, as it feeds solely on insects and fruit. A classic case of misrepresentation. That is not to say there aren't bloodsucking vampire bats—there are, though they comprise three distinct species that range from Mexico to Brazil, Chile, and Argentina. Suffice it to say that there is no evidence to suggest that they served as a basis for the creation of the vampire myths that spread through parts of medieval Europe. Belonging to the family of New World leaf-nosed bats (*Phyllostomidae*), they find shelter in hollow trees, among large palm leaves, in caves, or in buildings. These goggle-eyed, blood-sucking animals reach a maximum width of around thirteen inches with their wings wide-open; their fur is reddish or brown. They live in large flocks and their hearing is so keen they can detect the footfall of a cricket. The naturalist Alexander von Humboldt (1769–1859) gave this account of his personal experiences concerning these bats, in words only somewhat friendlier to bats than those of Conrad Gesner centuries earlier:

> Even when the heat of the sun is replaced by the chill of the night, the horses and the cattle cannot find a peaceful rest. As soon as these animals go to sleep, hideous bats come to suck their blood in the manner of vampires, clinging on their backs and leaving wounds that get covered by puss, attracting all manner of flies, horseflies, and other insects that lay their larvae inside. . . . Large bats flickered over our hammocks during most of the night, making us fear at any moment that they would hit our faces. . . . Not much later one of them . . . bit or, as the locals say, "stung" our dog on the nose. These bats had . . . a long tongue covered with wartlike projections, a highly efficient sucking device they can narrow considerably. The wound was small and round.

The dog howled loudly, clearly not so much from pain but, rather, fear.

Most species of blood-sucking bats resort to sucking blood only at times when food is otherwise scarce—in colder months, for example, when they are unable to find enough insects or fruit to live on. At these times the starving bats swarm out of their hiding places and set in the search of warm-blooded animals from which to draw enough nutrition for themselves. Naturalist-explorer Hermann Burmeister (1807–1892) described this phenomenon in his work on Brazil and Argentina:

> They devote themselves so avidly to sucking blood that they sometimes get discovered and caught by the sentries. I have no reliable information on whether they attack humans also, since I have yet to meet anyone who has been bitten by a vampire. The exact manner in which these bats suck blood is also unclear. All that can be known is that they sit on their victim with their wings half-open, push the fur apart, and just barely pressing their verrucose chins against the skin, they begin to suck the blood. The mark left behind is a small, shallow hole that is not at all similar to a typical puncture wound. I believe they suck up the skin first, then bite the tip of the swelling off with their sharp canine teeth. The bleeding that follows the bite is never too severe.

How, then, did myths come round to *linking* bats, humans, and the sucking of blood? One of the most common explanations cites legends that vampires appeared first on the earth not as humans, but in batlike form—monsters arriving from a hidden, evil world; creatures that took the form of bats primarily because they could effectively hide from humans' inquisitive eyes. These bats—or, rather, vampires—were long and wide but extremely thin. When flying, they looked just like bats, but on landing, their wings resembled extended human arms. Their bulgy, reddish eyes were the color of blood, whereas their furless, pale faces suggested the waxy appearance of dead humans.

New Caledonia Flying Fox (*Pteropus vetulus*). Created by Mesnel, published on Le Tour Du Monde, Paris, 1867.

Chapter 4

Werewolves

It was commonly held in Romanian villages for centuries that blood-sucking vampires could transform into wolves when in a fit of rage. Such vampires-turned-wolves tore their victims apart with unspeakable ferocity, leaving behind only scraps of flesh and puddles of blood. The origins of such legends are hard to trace, in part because these predatory, carnivorous animals—once common all over the European continent, are today rare (though Transylvania is still home to some). True, a self-respecting wolf may try its best to bite its victim's neck, but this is an act of efficiency (the prey is easier to kill that way) rather than one of cruelty—indeed, it is what allows them to swiftly fell quarry such as cattle, oxen, and horses that are much larger than themselves. Biting through the blood vessels in the neck makes the victims bleed profusely. And so it seems reasonable to conclude that this helped usher wolves into the realm of vampire mythology.

Wolves generally live in packs or groups, but some live and hunt individually; either way, in the days when their numbers were greater they caused considerable trouble to villagers by decimating livestock. This, then, yielded true or partially true stories that developed with time into mythical legends. In the majority of these legends the lonely wolf is characterized not only by its cruelty in killing, but also by a sinister intelligence. Its cleverness and might leaves unarmed humans powerless against them. According to some tales even magic is ineffective against such wolves. Yet another element linking wolves with vampire lore was their nocturnal ways, not to mention what to many villagers must have been spine-chilling howls. Interestingly enough, however, early vampire legends from Romania did not specify vampires as active at night like wolves. It took the Romantic era of the nineteenth century to complete the link and place them firmly in the realm of darkness.

Yet another ingredient in the mix of admiration and fear humans have long felt toward wolves is the close cooperation these creatures exhibit when hunting in packs. It is also worth mentioning that wolves were hard-pressed to find adequate food during some severe Eastern European winters, so they were occasionally known to enter more densely populated territories, seeking out livestock and, occasionally, happening upon humans, with unfortunate consequences for the two-legged being.

As various Eastern European legends recount, not only vampires, but also some humans, have the *were*withal to transform into wolves. Perhaps due to a developmental malformation, so the thinking went, such people were born with the capacity of becoming wolves whenever they feel an irresistible urge to, devouring animals (sheep and cattle) with a ferocity befitting a bona fide wolf. The good news was this: only if surprised at the moment of their transformation would they attack other humans.

WEREWOLVES THROUGH THE AGES

Werewolves were present as far back as the folklore of the Middle Ages, often in the form of fearsome apparitions that appeared in keeping with the cycles of the moon and went about infecting healthy bodies by biting them in vampiric fashion. As apparent from one written account from the annals of Transylvanian folklore, the presence of a werewolf was always sensed by the animals that were generally their victims:

A shepherd led his twelve oxen up a hillside, unaware that close by, deep in the forest, lurked three wolves that now began a stealthy approach. Though the person didn't see a thing, the oxen sensed that these predators were there, and on getting close enough, one of the oxen attacked the nearest wolf, piercing its side with its horn and lifting it into the air. But the wolf was so heavy that the ox set it back on the ground and let it run away. The next day a man was said to have died in the neighboring village, his side having been punctured by an ox. Thus it was proven that this man had been a werewolf.

A second human character with the ability to transform into an animal likewise occurred in such Romanian mythology: the *pricolici*. In contrast with werewolves, however, the pricolici was able to assume more than one shape. Most often they turned into dogs that commenced to kill all other, regular dogs nearby—but they could also transform into a wolf,

a cat, or even a frog. Most commonly however they appear in the shape of a yellow dog. The pricolici is recognizable from birth, since he comes to the world with long, pointy teeth protruding from his mouth, as well as a rudimentary tail. When assuming animal form, he turns incredibly aggressive, devouring any human being or animal that gets into his way. He is incredibly intelligent, strong, and violent, which makes any defense almost impossible. Thus ran one written account:

> The pricolici is at first a human being, but on doing three somersaults he turns into a yellow dog, a wolf, or a cat. The pricolici attacks, kills, and devours any human being it encounters. The sole way to render it powerless is to stab it and wait until its blood flows completely away, at which point the pricolici will vanish. But if even a drop of blood remains, the pricolici will return with a vengeance. If stabbed again, he will turn back into a human being, and if it avoids getting stabbed this time around, it will tear a human being into the smallest pieces.

In short, legend had it that a wounded pricolici which loses all its blood is rendered powerless, and thus turns back into a plain old human being. In no few Romanian villages during the Middle Ages, anyone bearing an unexplained scar was at risk of being accused of being a pricolici. Moreover, if these scars opened up frequently and were slow to heal, the unfortunate individual was presumed to be a still-active pricolici. In this event, with luck he or she could go on living, albeit as an outcast or, in the event that panic spread, be killed. And, as in the case of one village, postmortem measures were taken. A severe outbreak of plague followed an old woman's death. The brave men put their heads together, and someone reported having seen the woman in a dream in which it became clear that she had caused the plague. What to do? Soon word spread that her tomb had opened up, and of course her body was found in a different position than the one in which it had been interred; and so her heart was pierced with a nail and her body covered with a thorny bush that was then sprinkled with oil and set on fire. This finally put an end to the plague.

Chapter 5

Pellagra and Porphyria

There is an illness that seems tailor made for the cryptic world of vampire legends—namely, pellagra, whose symptoms were first described in Spain in 1735 by Gaspar Casal, who was eventually to earn the less than pleasant distinction of having the skin rash that appears on the necks of sufferers (who are exposed to sunlight) dubbed the "Casal collar." The condition, however, was not named by him, but by the Italian Francesco Frapoli in 1771. It was Frapoli who created a compound word of the elements *pelle* (skin) and *agra* (sour). Pellagra therefore means "rough skin." The disease reached epidemic proportions at the turn of the eighteenth and the nineteenth centuries. The cause of the illness long remained a mystery, but as science advanced, the most common hypothesis was that a microbe was to blame. Then along came Polish biochemist Casimir Funk (1884–1967), generally credited with first to formulate the concept of vitamins. He was likewise the first person to derive nicotinic acid from yeast, and through further research it was revealed in 1937 that pellagra was caused by a lack of nicotinic acid in the system. Later it also turned out that a lack of tripophane, an amino acid, also gave rise to such symptoms.

Why was the incidence of pellagra especially high in Serbia, Romania, Bulgaria, and Ukraine—not to mention some regions of Spain, Italy, France, and the United States? Because, as research was to show, in all of these regions, the poor consumed a diet almost wholly based on corn. Although corn does contain some amount of nicotinic acid, most of it is in a bound, hard-to-absorb form, and moreover, corn is low in tripophane. Why then did pellagra remain uncommon in Mexico, where corn is a staple food source? As determined later, because there corn was typically boiled for hours in milk of lime, and the heat treatment released the nicotinic acid.

Pellagra has three characteristic symptoms: dermatitis, diarrhea, and dementia. In the absence of treatment, their worsening condition ultimately leads to death. The skin of the afflicted becomes inflamed and discolored, in addition to peeling and being beset by hornification. Fine, but what was the presumed link between such poor souls and creatures of the night? Consider first that the symptoms—including the Casal collar—appeared in particular on those parts of the body exposed to sunlight, such as the face, the neck, and limbs. And such external symptoms were accompanied by a reddening or even ulceration of the mucous membrane in the mouth, as well as around the genitals and the anus. The most common gastric symptom was diarrhea, which was apt to include blood as the disease advanced, but nausea and vomiting also occurred. The consequent pressure on the nervous system led also to memory loss, disorientation, melancholy, stress, restlessness, and insomnia—and aggression. Eventually, the person would lose all of his or her mental capacity.

In short, then, the external lesions that afflicted pellagra sufferers, as well as the behavioral changes such persons often exhibited, brought to mind the image that common fantasy had built around vampires. As sunlight harms the skin of sufferers, they tried avoiding light altogether, which in turn imparted their skin over time with a yellowish white, parchmentlike hue.

To make matters worse, vampires were assumed to have awfully bad breath, and, indeed, pellagra patients often fared poorly in this respect as well due to the inflammation and bleeding going on in their mouths, not to mention their persistent nausea.

And, while there is no evidence to suggest that diarrhea ever conjured up an image of vampires in the popular imagination, the star player in at least one vampire legend is verminosis; that is to say, a disease or infestation caused by parasitic worms—which often leads to diarrhea.

To make matters even worse for pellagra sufferers, that's not where the similarities between them and blood-sucking creatures of the night ended. The oral inflammation led to appetite loss, which in turn led to weight loss. Well, it was commonly held that vampires don't consume regular food at all, just blood—which helps explain why Dracula never dines with his guests.

Symptoms akin to manic depression often accompanied pellagra, making it all the more likely that its sufferers lived up to the popular image of vampires. As everyone knew, after all, vampires did not sleep at night, either—and they are apt to be sulky and irritable. As for yet another parallel, it was commonly held that vampires would have a strong urge to visit any and all relatives they had unfinished business in the daytime hours with and bring them into temptation—it took just a bite, after all. As for pellagra sufferers, their relatives with similar nutritional habits often also came down with the disease—revenge taken by the sick person who had passed away? Finally, the gastric and intestinal bleeding those suffering from pellagra were so often subject to also served to conjure up images of the living dead.

From time to time, bodies were exhumed from their graves and given a thorough once-over to confirm that, indeed, they were vampires. On one occasion in the hinterlands of nineteenth-century Transylvania, an unspoiled corpse was rumored to have been found with rosy cheeks and fresh blood around its mouth. In yet another case, traces of corn-meal were found around the mouth of a dead person—surely proof that this pellagra sufferer had in fact been a vampire.

VAMPIRITIS

There is also another group of disorders that has been linked to a belief in vampires—namely, por-phyrias. Much less common than pellagra, porphyrias were finally traced to a gene mutation only in the late-twentieth century. In short, here, too, sufferers develop some characteristics befitting of vampires. They are highly sensitive to sunlight, with excessive exposure often causing skin discoloration and blisters. To further ensure their potential to be mistaken for crazed creatures of the night, the hair tends to grows thick on their faces and extremities; and their eyes water, as if from excitement at the prospect of going on the prowl (or having just returned). Add to this that they are prone to develop neurological abnormalities—and there you have it, a picture-perfect vampire.

Research was to show that porphyria symptoms could be triggered not only by sunlight but by certain chemicals as well—most aptly, those particularly found in garlic.

All this lends credence to suggestions by some scholars that porphyria may have played a notable role in the formation of vampire legends.

The gene at issue here, as modern-day research was to show, is responsible for coding the enzyme termed urod (uroporphyrinogen-decarboxilase), which has a key role in the body's biochemistry. Porphyria is, then, caused by a mutation of this gene that blocks the functioning of the enzyme, yielding an accumulation of uroporphyrin, which in turn activates on exposure to sunlight, causing the characteristic symptoms of the disease.

The only efficient known treatment: regular *blood* transfusion. Hm. It's a good thing that villagers centuries ago who feared for their blood didn't know that, in fact, these poor souls had even more in common with vampires than they ever imagined.

Chapter 6

Bloodletting

One of the most pervasive tenets of medieval medicine was that bodily fluids carried sickness, and that these fluids consequently had to be expelled from time to time to promote healing. The practice of doing so stretches back to Antiquity—namely, to the ancient Greeks' and Romans' theory of the humors, which were believed to disrupt the body's inner harmony if polluted or out of balance. To restore balance it was seen as sometimes necessary to rid the body of the excess body fluids. This was further based on observation of phenomena like sweating, spontaneous bleeding, or the formation of pus-filled blisters, which could be explained as the body's attempt to cleanse itself.

Antiquity had more than one method or, rather, route into the body when it came to such endeavors. Cleansing from the top meant swallowing an emetic to induce vomiting; from the bottom, the application of enemas or various purgatives, diuretics, and sudorifics (which cause or increase sweat). In some cases—gastric complaints or colic, for example—this could in fact lead to a bit of relief. It was not uncommon, though, that such otherwise well-intended medical intervention weakened an illness-stricken body so much that the patient died. The fear of fatal consequences led to less drastic treatments, including various diets.

Bloodletting was the most common of all medieval humor-cleansing procedures, applied to treat a broad range of conditions. Since blood was seen as the wellspring of life, it was thought that the majority of illnesses were caused by its deterioration. On this reasoning, polluted blood had to be let out to restore health. Generally a vein close to the skin was cut on the premise that the blood streaming out would drive toxic contaminants from the body, and otherwise help bodily fluids return to a healthy balance. At the same time, recovery from particular ailments was linked to specific veins. After making the diagnosis, however, the practitioner had to find

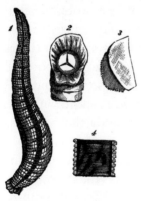

Medicinal leech or Hirudo medicinalis, vintage engraving. Trousset encyclopedia (1886–1891)

not only the right spot on the body to slice open a vein, but also the right time to do it. One key factor, of course, was choosing the right lunar phase. The moon was believed to make fluids expand, and so under this reasoning, the fuller it was and the stronger it shined, the more severe were the symptoms of illness.

Bloodletting could also be accomplished in a somewhat less invasive manner. This involved pressing glass cups upside-down against the skin and depleting the oxygen inside with a scrap of burning cloth. The resultant vacuum sucked blood from capillaries just under the skin. One variation involved placing the cups on an open wound in an effort to suck out puss and blood that was thought polluted.

Leeches (vampires of the worm world!) were also often applied. Typically a dozen or so were placed on an area of skin that had been cut, as necessary to facilitate their sucking of blood until satiated, perhaps for a half-hour or so. They then fell from the body; or, if not, they were rubbed with salt, which shrunk them and, importantly, their mouths, causing them in turn to release their grip. Science later discovered that the salvia of leeches contains a chemical that serves both to prevent clotting and keep a wound open longer. In the Middle Ages this phenomenon was seen as proof of a long-lasting healing effect.

Chapter 7
Blood Legends

It didn't take modern science for people to understand that blood is a precondition of human life. Thus it follows that important motifs of existence—birth and death, as well as age-old pursuits like hunting—have, since ancient times, been linked with the concept of blood. Since blood loss yields weakness and, ultimately, death, some ancient peoples came to imagine that drinking blood could restore vitality, or that the blood of the living had the power to resuscitate the dead. Blood was seen as a magic substance in almost all ancient cultures.

The examples are many. Central to the traditional religion of the Shilluk people, from along the White Nile in what is modern-day Southern Sudan, was an initiation ceremony that involved spreading a mixture of the blood and bile of a sacrificial animal, combined with water and saliva, on the skin of initiates while wrapping them in the animal's intestines. And in the traditional religion of the Bataks, a proto-Malay people in Sumatra, the dead were seen as foes of the living and commanded special respect. A variety of sacrificial rites were performed to keep their spirits at bay. It was further believed that the living car-

Aztec ritual human sacrifice

ried in their bodies a superior, otherworldly power called the tondi—which dwelled in the blood but whose force permeated one's entire physical being. Hence it was highly undesirable that even a hair from one's body, much less a drop of blood, should fall into the enemies' hands. Similarly, portions of a captured enemy would be eaten in the belief that doing so meant appropriating this force. On occasion, blood acquired thus was poured into bowls, to be later mixed into food.

HUMAN SACRIFICE

In the rites of the Aztecs, human sacrifices played a crucial role beyond their function as an offering to the god Acolnahuacatl. The sacrifice *itself* was considered a visage of the deity, and was indeed referred to by a term that meant, in essence, "divine image." During the ceremony several priests held the chosen person down on a sacrificial altar to allow the head priest, using an obsidian knife, to cut the still throbbing heart from the chest. The channels cut into the altar stone helped gather the flowing blood, this precious liquid, which served as the libation of their gods. How benign just a bite on the neck from a vampire of centuries to come might have seemed by comparison!

Perhaps the most complex belief system related to blood emerged among early civilizations of Central Asia and the Near East. In these myths blood appears as a substance carrying supernatural, divine powers. According to the Mesopotamian creation myth, the first man was made from mud mixed with the blood of a deity that other gods had sacrificed for this purpose. Having been created from divine blood meant that a share of this liquid of supernatural origin should be returned to the gods through sacrifices (and you thought that banks charged high interest rates!) Evil and destructive gods were particularly favored with blood sacrifices. Moloch, the destructive deity of Phoenicia, could only be appeased by sacrifices—originally human, with sheep later used as a substitute. The ceremonies took place in a valley called Gehenna, near Jerusalem, which became the name the Hebrews later used for hell.

The ancient Greeks believed that the blood of the gods, which they referred to as *ichor*, provided immortality and limitless energy. A single drop of a god's blood was enough for the creation and birth of new gods. A good example is the myth of Uranus, the god who married his own mother, Gaia, the goddess of fertility. Their union gave birth to a brood of gigantic monsters, each with a hundred arms or a single eye. Fearing his horrific offspring, Uranus had them exiled to the netherworld, or Hades. This made Gaia so furious that she had her children rebel against him under the direction of the titans. The youngest of the titans, Chronos, who was the god of time, put an end to his father's reign by cutting off Uranus's penis with a scythe. But watch out! A few drops of Uranus's blood then fell on Earth, giving birth to, among other creatures, the three Erinyes, the avenging Furies. Their waists are entwined with serpents, their black bodies are carried on bat wings anywhere in the world, their eyes drip with blood, and they lunge at their victims like ferocious dogs. The Furies inflict violent remorse upon those who have committed horrendous crimes, or otherwise trouble their thoughts until they are fully repentant of their sins; and, yes, they also torture sinners in the netherworld.

Greek mythology attributed powers not only to the blood of the gods but also to any kind of blood, regarding it as the source of the human soul. Blood was thus seen as a conduit to the spirits of the dead.

JUDEO-CHRISTIAN AND PAGAN BLOOD TRADITIONS

In traditional Jewish religious practice, anything connected with the name of God, or Jahve, was sacred, but might become impure if invoked in everyday life. Believers could never forget this were they to live pure lives and thus have an unhindered path to God after death. Since humans were a creation of Jahve, anything soiled with blood was regarded as impure. For this reason, Jews were prohibited from consuming food that might contain blood—hence, in part, the strict dietary rules adhered to by many orthodox Jews even today. And menstruation was seen as an impurity, too; so during their time of the month, women were not allowed to touch anything regarded as sacred or to appear in a sacred place—not that that the Jewish religion has been alone in this respect among the world's religions and cultures.

Christians likewise attribute a mystical importance to blood, of course. God, through the sacrifice of his only son, Jesus, is said to have redeemed humanity from original sin. Saint Justin

Martyr (100–165), who lived in the second century, writes in his apology to Emperor Antoninus (138–161) about the sacrificial ceremony commemorating the crucifixion of Christ and the bleeding of his wounds (the stigmas), called the Eucharist:

> Those who are called by us deacons give to each of those present to partake of the bread and wine mixed with water over which the thanksgiving was pronounced, and to those who are absent they carry away a portion. And this food is called among us the Eucharist, of which no one is allowed to partake but the man who believes that the things which we teach are true, and who has been washed with the washing that is for the remission of sins, and unto regeneration, and who is so living as Christ has enjoined. For not as common bread and common drink do we receive these; but in like manner as Jesus Christ our Savior, having been made flesh by the Word of God, had both flesh and blood for our salvation, so likewise have we been taught that the food which is blessed by the prayer of His word, and from which our blood and flesh by transmutation are nourished, is the flesh and blood of that Jesus who was made flesh.

In the ceremony of the Holy Communion each faithful symbolically consumes the flesh of Jesus with the bread (or sacred host), and receives his blood by drinking ceremonial wine.

BLOOD TIES AND THE HUNGARIANS

Blood ties were fundamental to the structure of the tribal societies that once thrived across the vast region sweeping from Inner Asia all the way to Eastern Europe. These peoples saw the magic power of blood as both a connection to the gods and that which—when two people united, representing that so very elemental (and most enjoyable) mixing of blood (and other bodily fluids)—made it possible for clans to survive and multiply. For protection, large families united into tribes, some of which entered into blood oaths to create larger alliances. This brings us to the Hungarians, aka the Magyars.

The seven Magyar tribes, in quest of a new land, tied a blood oath, as is told by legend: Each chieftain opened the vein of his arm with the tip of their sword, and let the escaping blood flow into a horn. A shaman took the horn. Holding it, he presented it first to the war chief, and then to Grand Prince Árpád, who took a drink from the horn, first savoring the common blood, and then passing it around. The six other chieftains took the horn in their turn and drank from the common blood. Chief Zoard poured what was left into the fire of the altar, the flames of which blazed cheerfully towards the high sky, towards the Lord of the Warfare.

This mystic unifying force of blood ties called

for the custom of blood revenge as well. The murder of a relative needed avenging. Blood could be washed away only with blood, meaning that the spirit of the victim could be appeased only by taking the life of another person, either the killer himself or one of his family members.

The popular folklore, legends, and tales of Eastern Europe preserve a great variety of the blood legends inherited from the tribal era. A drop of blood, in Hungarian folktales, often appears as a key ingredient of magical practices. Drops of blood that fall to earth can personify their owner, and are left behind sometimes intentionally by a character fleeing an enemy. Indeed, such drops can even speak in their owner's voice, thus confusing the pursuer.

Chapter 8

Blood Libels

The blood libels by which the persecution of Jews was justified for many across Europe for centuries are perhaps the most widespread blood-related myths history has seen. The common allegation: on the occasion of Passover some Jews would kill Christians, often children, in sacrificial rituals and mix their blood into the matzos they prepared for this week-long holiday.

Prejudice against the Jews began taking shape discernibly as early as Antiquity, in the period following the death of Alexander the Great (356–323 BC). Its roots at the time stemmed in part from the fact that the strictly monotheistic Jews did not accept the Hellenistic monarchs as deities and so refused to participate in their ceremonies. Indeed, the first documented case of a Jewish blood libel is found in a source written by Apion of Alexandria: "It was reported to King Aniochos that the Jews kept a Greek man captive in the temple, and after fattening him for an entire year, sacrificed him." Prejudices and related accusations against Jews grew during the Roman Empire.

Jews and Christians alike left the Middle East during this period, dispersing far and wide. The pagan priests of ancient Rome did not always differentiate between Jews and Christians, and indeed sources from the second century, for example, testify that blood libels were brought against Christians as well. The early Christian author Tertullian—known as "the father of Latin Christianity" and "the founder of Western theology"—complained in one of his writings that the members of his church were often accused of killing and eating infants. In the case of the Christians, the turning point came with the ascendance to the throne of Constantine the Great (307–337 ad), who, by his decree of religious tolerance, helped the Christians achieve a dominant position over pagan religions across the Roman Empire.

But the accusations against the Jews gained even more force.

Following the collapse of the Roman Empire, through the first centuries of the Middle Ages, Jewish communities still lived in relative peace. The leaders and the inhabitants of the Christian-feudal states, however, preferred to keep them at a distance, forcing them to live in separate districts or ghettos, or to wear pieces of yellow cloth on their garments.

Not being allowed to own land, many Jews worked instead in manufacturing or commerce. The blood libels that had originated in Antiquity remained repressed for centuries, but prejudices against Jews were now mounting anew. The blood libels were back with a vengeance in the era of the Crusades, starting in 1095.

THE FIRST BLOOD LIBEL

The first major blood libel in the Middle Ages was recorded in Norwich England, in 1144. The allegation was leveled by a converted Jew named Theobald, who may have been trying to improve his own standing among the Christians. He claimed that the region's Jews annually drew lots to choose which of their religious communities would get the task of ritually killing a Christian child. As proof, Theobald cited the disappearance of a boy called William, alleging he had been kidnapped, tortured, and killed by Jews. The whole thing seemed so far-fetched that no one was arrested and no lawsuit was brought, but nevertheless the story continued to flourish by word of mouth, returning blood libels against the Jews to the common consciousness.

Spreading accusations of blood libel had the effect and, perhaps, often the purpose, of chasing the Jews away from certain territories, though initially these fabrications did not put their lives at risk. The most famous cases were recorded in Gloucester, England (1168); Blois, France (1182); Saragosa, Spain (1182); and Winchester, England (1192). These blood libels claimed that the Jews committed their ritual killings by somewhat imitating the scenes of the Passion, methodically torturing kidnapped children before crucifying them.

It wasn't long before blood libel had deadly consequences for the accused. In 1255, a boy called Hugh disappeared in Lincoln, England. A rumor alleged that a local Jewish community had held him captive for ten days, fattening him on milk and bread, before crucifying him. An investigation followed, and subsequently eighteen Jews were put to death.

The details of such cases show, however, that while these early cases can be termed blood libels, they were more about alleged human sacrifices and ritual killings, but without according a major role to the motive of taking blood.

BLOOD LIBEL IN THE RENAISSANCE AND BEYOND

From the fifteenth to the seventeenth centuries a gradual change unfolded in the character of the blood libels. The main accusation against the Jews became the assumption that they needed Christian blood for their unleavened bread. These allegations overlooked the fact that traditional Jewish religious practice strictly prohibited the consumption of any food soiled with blood. The blood libels that became widespread in German territories claimed that the Jews used the Christian blood not only for ritual purposes, but also in medication, as an element of healing, and in magic potions. Rumors of such supposed incidents spread far and wide across Europe thanks in particular to traveling priests and Jesuit monks.

Of course, the Inquisition likewise played a decisive role in investigating such blood libels and, indeed, persecuting Jews as a result. The renowned Spanish inquisitor Tomás de Torquemada (1420–1498) accused the entire Jewish community of the Castilian city of La Guardia, cruelly tormented its members, and sentenced most of them to be burned on the stake. His vigorous anti-Jewish campaign culminated in 1492 with the expulsion of all Jews from Spain.

By the end of the fifteenth century, hatred against the Jews flared up once again. Following an infamous blood libel in the Italian city of Trento, a boy by the name of Simon—a boy who had disappeared and, so it was claimed, had fallen victim to the local Jews—eventually became a saint. The official veneration by Catholics of Saint Simon of Trent ended only in 1965, when the Vatican finally eliminated his name from the list of saints, pronouncing the blood libel unfounded.

While the Jewish communities of Europe represented the largest group of victims over the centuries, at times other ethnic and religious groups were likewise subjected to blood libels. In all cases, though, the core notion was this: blood was a mystical substance, one whose power was no less than it had been in our tribal days.

Depiction of the alleged killing of Simon of Trent

Part II
Dracula and History

Chapter 9

Three Principalities

The history of vampirism is more than tales of gore and persecution. To fully understand how the world's most famous vampire, and the imitations and permutations he spawned came to be, we must also pay heed to the very ground he rose from; by this we mean the three principalities most closely tied to history's alpha vampire: Count Dracula.

The legends surrounding the vampire race and the figure of Dracula are most commonly tied to Transylvania, but the two neighboring historic territories of Wallachia and Moldavia also have major roles to play. The original vampire myth was rooted elsewhere, but it was in these three principalities that it became a strong superstition and a popular cultural tradition. Over time these traditions evolved and were enriched with new elements, and they survive to this day as a living heritage—or, in some cases, they are kept alive and nurtured for commercial reasons.

The three regions that Vlad the Impaler, the historical Dracula, had ties with by and large developed their cultural traditions individually. It was only in 1861 that Wallachia and Moldavia united under the name Romania, and it was after World War I that Transylvania, taken away from the historical Hungary that had lost World War I, found itself part of Romania as well.

A BRIEF HISTORY OF TRANSYLVANIA

Immediately to the east of present-day Hungary and today situated in Romania, the largely mountainous region known as Transylvania, meaning "the land beyond the forest," was from the time of the Hungarian conquest culturally and politically distinct from the Hungarian (Magyar) tribal federation whose rule swept much of the Carpathian Basin starting with the Magyar Conquest of 896. Later, during the first three centuries of the Kingdom of Hungary, under the ruling House of Árpád (1000–1301), Transylvania became a separate principality altogether—ruled by the prince who was heir to the Hungarian throne. Although this system did not survive the demise of the Árpád dynasty, even afterward Transylvania never did fully assimilate administratively or otherwise into Hungary; rather, it preserved its separate standing and was led by governing princes appointed by monarchs.

By the thirteenth century, the Transylvanian princes were counted as among the most distinguished Hungarian aristocrats and military leaders, and remained as such through the fifteenth century; for not only did they govern a large geographical area—mostly following their own best judgment—but led the country's most important military force. The defense lines on the eastern and southern borders of Hungary followed the long, concentric, curvy, and thickly forested ranges of the Carpathian Mountains. They were vital indeed, since from the eleventh and twelfth centuries, successive waves of invading forces arrived from regions further east, including Asia. Through the eleventh century, the Cumans—who occupied the land spreading between the western coast of the Black Sea and the lower reaches of the Danube—stormed their way into Transylvania on more than one occasion. Their territory, Cumania, was also home to Slavic land-laborers who lived under their occupation and to the Vlachs, who had migrated to this area and were to be known as Romanians from the nineteenth century onward.

The Vlachs, under foreign occupation from the end of the Middle Ages, drew their numbers from the southern parts of the Balkans. The first of their settlers might have arrived in the eleventh century to the territory later known as Wallachia, under Bulgarian rule at the time, extending from the southern Carpathians to the lower reaches of the Danube. During their cohabitation with the southern Slavs, the Vlachs assimilated many of their customs. The continuing yet hopeless fight of the Bulgarian state against Byzantium led to the weakening of Bulgaria, giving the Vlachs a chance to create their own organizational units, while keeping up the appearance of dependence. These tribal units were ruled by chieftains referred to in various Slavic languages as *knyaz*. Gradually, these "knyazdoms" merged and led to the formation of the voivodeships in Wallachia and Moldavia, with their leading class of tenants-in-chief called boyars. With the eleventh-century collapse of the Old Bulgarian Empire, the Vlach knyazdoms and voivodeships lacked the power to preserve their independence and were subsequently overrun by the Cumans, arriving from the east.

A BRIEF HISTORY OF WALLACHIA AND MOLDAVIA

Shortly before the Mongol invasion that decimated Hungary and its population in 1241–1242, the Cumans sought refuge in Hungary, leaving the Vlachs under the power of the Mongols' khanate known as the Golden Horde. Once the Golden Horde disbanded, the Vlachs once more grasped at an opportunity for independence. The Wallachian knyazdoms and voivodeships were united under Basarab I (c. 1310/1319–1352), who rose to become the ruling voivode (or prince) of Wallachia. In 1324, he also attempted to extend his rule to the Banat of Severin—a political, military, and administrative unit of the Kingdom of Hungary. This provoked a full-scale assault from Charles I, King of Hungary (1288–1342), the ultimate failure of which preserved Wallachia's independence. Basarab's son, Nicholas Alexander I (r. 1352–1363), had to face later battle campaigns by Louis the Great of Hungary and Croatia (1326–1382). These called for an alliance, which was established with the southern Slavic powers Serbia and Bulgaria as they split from the Byzantine Empire—an alliance bound up with the Eastern Orthodox Church. Moreover, in retaliation against attempts at proselytization issuing from Roman Catholic Hungary, Nicholas Alexander I founded the Wallachian Eastern Orthodox Metropolitan Seat.

The territory of the future Moldavia was held under the rule of the Tatars for longer than Wallachia—up until mid-fourteenth century. Soon after the Tatar withdrawal, a new political field of power emerged, with Moldavia threatened by the Poles from the north and the Hungarians from the west. Emerging as the victor, Louis the Great managed to hold Moldavia in tenure. His liege in command, the voivode Dragoș, faced rebellion and eventual expulsion by Bogdan in 1365, who took the voivode's place and declared himself sovereign of independent Moldavia. His heir, Lacko, couldn't retain his independence and was forced to swear allegiance to Louis the Great, who had since also become King of Poland.

In the late-fourteenth century, there appeared on the southern frontier a sweeping new threat—the Ottoman Turks. The Battle of Kosovo in 1389 signified a catastrophic defeat for the Serbs. Even though the Ottoman forces were also decimated in the battle, the Serbs were compelled to appeal for Hungarian stewardship of their remaining northern lands.

In 1396, in response to a petition from Bulgaria, Hungarian king Sigismund of Luxemburg (1368–1437) gathered his army of mercenaries and attempted to roust the Turks out of the Balkans, but was thwarted at the Battle of Nikopol. This turn of events ultimately left Bulgaria under Turkish rule. Another result was that advancing Turkish forces reached the southern stretch of the Danube River, directly threatening Wallachia.

King Sigismund thus aimed to prevent the Turkish breach of southern Hungarian borders by conquering and controlling Wallachia. Although the Wallachian ruler Mircea the Elder (1355–1418) had proved strong enough to resist Hungarian and Turkish bids for hegemony, his successors had to accede to Hungarian stewardship. The continual military success of the Hungarian Hunyadi family against the Turks guaranteed at least limited autonomy for Wallachia, but during the Hungarian kingdom's decline at the beginning of the sixteenth century, Wallachia was forced to become an established Turkish tributary.

Moldavia's situation was even more complicated than that of Wallachia. The voivode Stephen the Great of Moldavia (1433–1504) took the throne in 1457 and reinforced his state against Hungarian, Polish, and Turkish conquest. His successor, voivode Peter IV Rareș (c. 1487–1546), went on to

Schedelsche Weltchronik or *Nuremberg Chronicle* Wallachia illustration (1493, Hartmann Schedel)

suffer military defeats from all three neighboring opponents. A series of successful Turkish campaigns against Hungary between the years 1526 and 1541 also sealed the fate of Moldavia, which was compelled to pay tribute to the Turks in 1538. Moldavia and Wallachia went on to become highly autonomous Turkish principalities. This status also applied to Transylvania, which was separated from Hungary by Turkish force. John Sigismund Zápolya (1540–1571) became the first Prince of Transylvanian and ruler of a part of the Kingdom of Hungary in 1570.

THE RISE OF THE VLADS

The ruling dynasty of Wallachia was founded by Basarab I and was henceforth known as the House of Basarab. Succession to the Wallachian throne, however, was not guided by the right of the firstborn to inherit an entire estate, as in Western European tradition; instead, the boyars retained the right to select which Basarab voivode, or prince, they saw fit for accession to the throne. Due to rampant rivalries and infighting, voivodes succeeded each other quite rapidly on the Wallachian throne. By the end of the fourteenth century, the House of Basarab had split in two; the descendants of the voivode Dănești constituting one line (the House of Dănești), while the progeny of the voivode Mircea the Elder comprised the other (the House of Drăculeşti—henceforth "Dracul" or "Dracula"). Even while the country's independence was under threat from neighboring powers, a struggle for power between the two clans arose. Vlad II, son of Mircea the Elder, was exiled to Transylvania, but he in turn convinced Sigismund of Luxemburg, king of Hungary, to aid his return to the throne. In 1436, already bearing the sobriquet Dracul, Vlad II won back the throne after murdering his rival of the Dăneşti lineage. His son, Vlad III, who was later dubbed Ţepeş (or the Impaler), ruled Wallachia in three separate periods: for a short spell in 1448 with Turkish aid, then backed as voivode by Hungary between 1456 and 1462, and finally again gaining the throne with Hungarian help in 1475, this time for a mere two months.

It was Vlad III who was later fashioned by rumor and legend into the bloodsucking vampire, Count Dracula.

Although these Eastern European peoples—the Hungarians and Romanians—sought consolation in Christianity amid the torments of continuous war, the manifold difficulties and suffering that defined their lives left its mark on that realm of their psyche. They felt that evil forces were ever present, trying to deprive them not only of their modest resources but also of their very lives and souls.

Hence, the folklore of these Eastern European nations depicted the world around them—an often incomprehensible and terrifying world—in even darker colors. Legends were born about such supernatural beings as ghosts, fairies, and devils, and transitional beings—such as werewolves and vampires— wandering on the border of this world and the world beyond. Yet other beliefs attributed supernatural capacities to humans, some of whom thus came to be viewed as witches, necromancers, or warlocks.

Chapter 10
The Fortresses of Sighişoara
and Bran

This brings us to the vampires' first—or at least—most successful translation from folklore into popular culture. Bram Stoker's novel *Dracula* personified the legend in the person of a Transylvanian count, living (or at least residing) among the mysterious Carpathian Mountains. Thanks to the popularity of Stoker's work, by the twentieth century Dracula's name became bound up in the common consciousness with that of the province of Transylvania, which until 1918 was under Hungarian rule and has since been part of Romania (with the exception of 1940–47, when its northern part was back with Hungary). It is worth examining the truths and misperceptions that have tied the historical Dracula with certain Transylvanian locations, namely the towns of Sighişoara (Segesvár in Hungarian, Schässburg in German) and Bran (Törcsvár in Hungarian, Törzburg in German).

The year 1437—the final year of the reign of Hungary's Sigismund of Luxemburg, who was also the Holy Roman Emperor—saw the so-called Union of Three Nations in Transylvania. Essentially an alliance between the nobility (i.e., mostly ethnic Hungarian vassals of the Hungarian king), the Szeklers (another group of Hungarians, who were primarily soldiers and frontier guards), and Saxon (ethnic German) burghers, this pact aimed initially to subdue a peasant rebellion. Even after it had registered its desired effect, however, it continued as a lasting class alliance determining Transylvania's social and political clime for centuries to come.

The Szeklers and Saxons lived in autonomous but legally administered districts—so-called *szék* in Hungarian and *Stuhl* in German, or seats—of Transylvania that fell beyond the jurisdiction of Hungarian royal counties. Even at the time of the founding of the medieval Kingdom of Hungary, in the year 1000, Szeklers had populated the eastern fringe of Transylvania, and the Saxons settled the region from the twelfth century on—establishing several major towns in southern Transylvania, including (Hermannstadt in German, Nagyszeben in Hungarian), Brașov (Kronstadt in German, Brassó in Hungarian), and Sighișoara.

Even during the reign of King Sigismund,

however, other peoples also inhabited Transylvania. The north had been settled by Slavs, and the southern and central areas were home to an increasing number of Romanians fleeing from the oncoming Turkish invasion of the Balkans. As the Slavs and Romanians were of Eastern Orthodox faith, a religion not recognized by the Hungary's Roman Catholic kingdom, they were forbidden to build churches (with rare exceptions) and their right to possess land was curtailed, so they lacked the means to participate in Hungarian politics by way of their own noble class.

Nevertheless, under King Sigismund's fiefdom policy, several prominent (knyaz and boyar) Romanian families of Wallachian extraction were granted considerable estates, mostly in Transylvania. These fiefdoms were granted with a definite political agenda. Turkish forces had been making continual headway into the northern Balkans, and they posed an increasing threat. Stuck between Hungary and the Ottoman Empire, Wallachia's political elite had two factions: one expecting Hungarian rule to ward off the Ottoman threat, the other opting for peace and stability through submitting to Turkish authority. King Sigismund was of course bent on supporting the pro-Hungarian faction, and they were, in turn, those to whom Sigismund granted fiefdom in Transylvania.

This is the backdrop to which the man who would be the inspiration for the fictional Dracula—Vlad III—came to prominence. Vlad III, who was later dubbed Țepeș (or the Impaler), ruled Wallachia (*not* Transylvania) in three periods: for a short spell in 1448 with Turkish aid, then backed as voivode by Hungary between 1456 and 1462, and finally again gaining the throne with Hungarian help in 1475, for a mere two months. It was Vlad III who was later reimagined as the bloodsucking vampire, Count Dracula.

DRACULA IN SIGHIŞOARA

Vlad II, or Vlad Dracul ("Vlad the Dragon") (c. 1393–1447)—who had been deposed from his Wallachian princely throne by the region's pro-Turkish faction—was granted an estate in Sighişoara, on the Târnava Mare River (Grosse Kokel in German, Nagy-Küküllő in Hungarian), by Hungary's King Sigismund. It was in there, in the fortress of Sighişoara, that the world's most famous alleged vampire, Vlad III, came unto this world.

The Vlad family and Sighişoara's Saxon burghers didn't quite see eye to eye, the latter fearing for their independence, and probably not without reason. Sighişoara was partly situated on a steep

Main entrance of the
Sighişoara fortress

precipice overlooking the fast-flowing river, and according to archive records, the fortress was first constructed under the reign of Hungarian king Géza II (1130–1162), whereas construction of the Upper Town and extended citadel district, with its fortified walls, was only begun around 1280. The Saxon burghers called the settlement Schässburg, and Hungary's Louis the Great had elevated it to town status in 1367. This period saw the completion of the fortress wall, as well as the erection of major church and secular buildings. The narrow alleys hemmed between the gothic town houses still exist, evoking a medieval atmosphere.

Dracula's house of birth stands to this day, right next to the citadel gate, beside the famous Clock Tower. The two-storey house isn't much to look at, really; nowadays it's a restaurant. Inside, small windows let in but a little light through the thick walls, affording a narrow view of a Saxon church. It is unclear just how long the future Vlad III resided under this particular roof, but the edifice is nonetheless a standing monument to Dracula's childhood—a childhood that would have a profound impact on his relations with the area commoners.

THE BRAN CASTLE IN BRAŞOV

Leaving Sighişoara and the Târnava Mare River and journeying southward to Braşov, we continue up the southern Carpathian slopes before finally reaching the little town of Bran. Saxon masons built the castle of Bran in 1377 by commission from Hungarian King Louis the Great, and later it was to play an important role in the defense against the Turks. Its ownership was passed on several times during the fifteenth century, until it finally ended up the property of the town of Braşov.

Legend has it that this castle served as a refuge for the same Vlad III, or Dracula, who acquired the Wallachian throne with Hungarian help and was subsequently banished back to Transylvania. Not that there is any substantial evidence of this. Nevertheless, popular belief has long had it that the imposing gothic castle, which looms out of the bluish mists of the snow-capped Carpathians, was the

Bran Castle

scene of unspeakable acts of terror perpetrated by its one-time resident, Dracula.

Indeed, the howling of wolves jarring the town's tranquility, and a sizable and nearby bear population, render this graceful and truly romantic castle all the more mystical. This storybook setting has long made Bran Castle a popular setting of vampire movies. When Romania took over Transylvania in 1918, Brașov handed ownership of Bran Castle over to Mary, queen of Romania. In 1937, the castle was inherited by her daughter, Princess Ileana, who later emigrated to the United States, where she died in 1991. The castle was appropriated by the Communist regime, though descendants of the former Romanian royal family have not formally renounced their claim to the property.

Chapter 11

Vlad the Impaler,
the Historical Dracula

Vlad the Impaler, the man who has gone down in history as the "real" Dracula, was born in Transylvania—then part of Hungary—around 1428–29, or maybe, if other sources are right, in 1431. At this time his father, Vlad II, who was a scion of the reigning dynasty of the principality of Wallachia, was living there in exile. He chose to remain in Transylvania because it shared a border with Wallachia to the south, and in his exile he contrived to return to his land as the reigning monarch. His sojourn in Transylvania allowed him to create an alliance with the Hungarian king of the time, Sigismund of Luxemburg, in the hope that with his help he could get rid of his rival on the throne.

Sighișoara—the birthplace of the historical Dracula—was a flourishing town thanks to the German-speaking Saxon merchants and craftsmen who inhabited it. But we know little indeed of the childhood years of Vlad the Impaler. The house in Sighişoara—still standing—where he is assumed to have be born seems to indicate that despite his exalted origins, he grew up more like common folk. Given the horrific acts he committed against city dwellers and especially merchants much later, during his years of reign, it might be fair to presume that his family's cohabitation of his family with the Saxon burgers was not quite friendly.

DRACULA IN HIS YOUTH

What we know of Vlad the Impeller's family background is that his mother—whose name was lost to time—was the daughter of a Transylvanian nobleman. Three sons were born from her marriage with Lad's father, Vlad II: the first was named Mircea; Vlad came second; and the third was Rado, later nicknamed Rado "the Handsome." The education of the children, in their early years, fell to their mother, and it must have followed the usual upbringing of noble youth.

Vlad II, Dracula's father, managed to regain the throne of Wallachia in 1436 and returned there with his family. At the time his son the future vampire was growing up, his father's throne was constantly in jeopardy and could only be kept through resource-ful—or, more aptly, cunning—political maneuvering. He had to feign allegiances to please both the Hungarians and the Turks, who were equally eager to expand their power over his country; and at the same time he had to address internal opposition from the region's wealthy boyars.

Vlad II was officially a vassal of the Hungarian monarch, and as a member of the Order of the Dragon, he was expected to fight with all his might to fend off the advance of the "faithless." His father, Mircea the Elder, was bound at this time to pay taxes to the Turks, and eventually Vlad II had to do the same, though as a vassal of the King of Hungary he shouldn't have been forced to pay taxes to anyone else. Vlad If's efforts to maintain independence became impossible, however, when Hungary's political and military power fell into the hands of the great strategist Janos Hunyadi, as the sweeping advance of the Turks reached the line of the Danube.

THE TURKS INVADE

In 1442 the Turks launched a campaign against Hungary, and their troops got as far as Alba Iulia (Gyulafehérvár in Hungarian; Weissenburg, later Karlsburg in German), in the center of Transylvania. When the armed conflict erupted, Vlad II tried remaining neutral so neither party could call him a traitor. This strategy backfired, however, and both sides accused him of treason. The Turkish troops suffered a sweeping defeat near Alba Iulia by the Hungarian army and were forced to leave Transylvania. Pursuing the retreating Turks, János Hunyadi soon entered Wallachia, removed Vlad II from his throne, and installed in his place Basarab II (r: 1442–1443), who was seen by the Hungarians as more loyal. Together with his family, Vlad II found refuge in Moldavia and immediately started plotting to get back the throne. Turning openly against Hungary, he vowed an alliance with the Turks. In 1443 Turkish troops entered Wallachia and chased Basarab II away.

Vlad II would be allowed take the throne back, but only at the price of signing a pledge making him a vassal of the Sultan. He committed himself to pay a yearly tax, which also included annually contributing a certain number of boys to train as soldiers for the Turks. Although Vlad II reclaimed the throne with Turkish help, based on their previous interactions the Turks did not trust him fully. As his status became uncertain again, he tried to firm up his position in 1444 by sending his two younger sons, Vlad and Radu, to the court of the Sultan as hostages—a proof of his loyalty. The young Vlad was around the age of fourteen when he arrived with his younger brother in the Ottoman court, where they would stay until 1448.

In 1443, Ulászló, King of Hungary (1424–1444), together with János Hunyadi, led a successful campaign against the Turks. After a series of defeats Sultan Murad II Kodja (1404–1451) sued for peace, offering in exchange huge swaths of territory along the banks the Danube. But Pope Eugene IV (1383–1447), in the hopes of chasing the Turks entirely out of territory of the Balkans, convinced the hotheaded young Hungarian ruler, Ulászló, to break the peace and start a new campaign against the Turkish Empire. Ulászló did so in 1444, again with the participation of János Hunyadi, and advanced with his troops all the way to the shore of the Black Sea. Upon starting the new campaign, János Hunyadi summoned Vlad II to enter the war against the Turks, in the spirit of a pledge he had made when entering the Order of the

Vlad the Impaler

Dragon. Vlad II tried to dodge the request by admitting to his pledge to the Sultan. In response, Pope Eugene IV released him from that pledge, putting him between a rock and a hard place, as his sons were still living among the Turks. Trying another maneuver, he sent his older son Mircea to war at the head of a smaller army. The misgivings Vlad II had concerning the fate of the campaign proved to be well founded. The Christian troops suffered a catastrophic defeat in the battle of Varna, which took the life of King Ulászló. János Hunyadi, who returned to a Hungary without a king, was elected regent (c. 1407–1456)—with the expectation of mounting yet another campaign against the Turks.

THE DEATH OF VLAD II

From the time that the battle of Varna was lost, János Hunyadi harbored a strong animosity against Vlad II and his older son Mircea, who in turn blamed him for the defeat. As a regent, János Hunyadi could exercise most of the rights of a crowned king, and he used this power to get rid of Vlad II. It is speculated that he was behind the plot when the boyars of Wallachia conspired in 1447 and killed both Vlad II and his older son, Mircea (who was blinded and buried alive). Following this, János Hunyadi installed

Vladislav II, a prince loyal to him. Upon the news of the assassination of Vlad II, the court of the Sultan decided to release his two sons, hoping they could be used against the Hungarians. With Turkish help, the young Vlad attacked Wallachia in 1448, chased Vladislav II away, and occupied the throne. His first reign lasted only two months, however; for János Hunyadi entered Wallachia as soon as the Turkish troops left. Vlad III was forced to escape, and Vladislav II returned to power.

After the Hungarian attack, Vlad III sought refuge with his cousin Bogdan, prince of Moldavia. During his exile, a dramatic event occurred that shook the entire Christian world: Constantinople fell at the hands of the Turks. With the occupation of the city in 1453, the more than thousand-year-old Byzantine Empire ceased to exist, and the center of the Orthodox Church was lost. The Court of the Sultan relocated there, and the city was renamed Istanbul. Right after this event, which shook all of Europe, Sultan Mehmed II "the Conqueror" (1432–1481) began plotting a campaign against Hungary.

Vlad III lived in exile under the protection of his cousin Bogdan until 1454, when a civil war erupted in Moldavia and Bogdan was killed. Forced yet again to flee, he faced the choice of seeking refuge on Turkish or Hungarian territory. He must have decided that Hungary was the lesser evil, for

he returned to Transylvania. This was a lucky decision. Vladislav II, thus far loyal to the Hungarians,
had meanwhile initiated a Turkish-friendly policy,
which János Hunyadi did not take kindly to at all.
Under the circumstances Hunyadi pardoned Vlad
III, whom he had previously regarded as his enemy,
and sought to use him as a tool against Vladislav II.

In 1456 Mehmed II led his army to the
southern fringes of Hungary, and on July 4 undertook the Siege of Belgrade. The captain defending
the fort—Mihály Szilágyi, the brother-in-law of
János Hunyadi—managed to hold off the Turks
until Hunyadi arrived with his army. In the meantime Hunyadi, fearing a complete turnaround in
Wallachia, promised military forces to Vlad III—
helping him to return to Wallachia, kill Vladislav II,
and seize power.

On July 22, Hunyadi won a resounding victory over the Turks—a landmark event that largely
halted the Ottoman advance into Catholic Europe
for seventy years.

But Hunyadi died shortly thereafter, in an
outbreak of plague.

On getting news of Hunyadi's death, Vlad III
took advantage of the temporary inertia of his Hungarian neighbors by seeking peace with the Turkish court to reinforce his position. Still recovering
after the major defeat, Mehmed II made a show of

accepting the offer.

Vlad III meanwhile set out to settle his scores with the boyars of Wallachia, punishing with unthinkable ruthlessness all those who questioned his power. He impaled all his enemies, earning the nickname Vlad "the Impaler."

His reign at the helm of Wallachia lasted from 1456 to 1462. It was during this time that his cruelties earned him his monstrous reputation. After his relationship with the Sultan deteriorated, Turkish attacks along the borders became a common occurrence, and Vlad III repelled them with an outstanding degree of military acumen. Ironically, this also earned him the reputation as a heroic defender of Christianity.

Under the constant menace of the Turks, Vlad the Impaler was obliged to accept help from the Hungarian king Matthias Corvinus (1443–1490), which meant that he also had to accept becoming his vassal. Looking to capitalize on his victories, Vlad undertook a campaign of his own, which proved initially successful because he treated the captured enemy with his usual brutality. It was doomed to fail, though, because his military power was insufficient, and he received little material support from Matthias. The Sultan, of course, did not forget the campaign and prepared to get rid of Vlad the Impaler.

In 1462 a new Turkish force invaded the territory of Wallachia and easily removed Vlad the Impaler from power. Yet again, Vlad had no other choice but to retreat to Transylvania. Tragically, his first wife committed suicide to avoid becoming a Turkish captive.

VLAD THE IMPALER IN CAPTIVITY

After crossing the Carpathian Mountains to reach Transylvania, Vlad the Impaler requested help from Matthias. The Hungarian king, however, decided to arrest him instead and have him held captive in his castle in Buda (i.e., on the hilly, Buda side of modern-day Budapest). Although the king's motivation for arresting a defender of Christianity and an ally remains unclear, it is a fact that the captivity of Vlad III lasted twelve years. Sources show that his imprisonment couldn't have been too uncomfortable; it was akin to house arrest, and the "house" was the king's castle. Reportedly Vlad III could enter the royal court freely, and he was even allowed to marry a female member of the royal family. One source falsely asserts that the wife of Vlad III was King Matthias's own sister. But this is so much ancient tabloid fodder, as Matthias never had a sister, and certainly would have forbid the marriage of any close relative to the bloodthirsty Vlad III. That Vlad III married at all is only hearsay, as no reliable source registers the name of the second wife, though several claim that Vlad III had two sons from that alleged marriage.

VLAD RETURNS, AND LOSES HIS HEAD

During the time of Vlad III's captivity, the throne of Wallachia was occupied by his brother Radu, who reigned as an ally of the Hungarian king. After some time he, too, was obliged to also split allegiances, under renewed Turkish pressure. Wanting to put an end to attacks on his territory, he placed his land under Turkish protection in the hope of finding stability and peace. After some hesitation, Matthias Corvinus responded to this by setting Vlad III free, and supporting him in a campaign to take back the Wallachian throne.

Due to Radu's sudden death, however, the war between brothers did not come to pass. In 1476 Vlad the Impaler invaded Wallachia for the third time — this time with help from the Prince of Transylvania, István Báthory, and Stefan the Great, Prince of Moldavia. Vlad III occupied the throne once again. After this successful campaign the Moldavian and Transylvanian armies departed, leaving only a couple of weeks for Vlad III to draft armed support inside his own country to ward off imminent Turkish attack. But the memory of his past cruelties kept the boyars at a distance. The peasantry, weary of the sacrifices frequent war campaigns had asked of them, was not willing to follow him, either. In December 1476, Vlad the Impaler thus faced the Turkish army with only a handful of soldiers. Defeat was inevitable. Indeed, he himself fell in battle. His head was subsequently cut off, preserved in honey, and sent to Sultan Mehmed II as a gift.

Chapter 12

Will the Real Dracula Please Stand Up?

Vlad the Impaler was by all accounts a brutal leader, filled with what we might term "bloodlust," but whether he can be dubbed the "original Dracula" remains a point of contention among historians and vampire enthusiasts alike.

Researchers have differing views as to who can be rightfully regarded as the historic inspiration for Dracula. The crux of the dispute often hinges on the question of just whom Bram Stoker modeled the main character of his world-famous novel on. Some of the uncertainty may stem from confusion about the names of the princes of Wallachia.

In medieval Europe, every individual kept track of his own line of ancestry, and therefore family names were not commonly used, only first (Christian) names. Since the same name could occur more than once in the same family, epithets were also used to differentiate between people, some of which referred to age (e.g., young or old); some to professions (e.g., tailor, smith, shepherd); yet others to size or hair color (e.g., small, blond, black). Members of the nobility commonly attached the names of their estates to their own names. Monarchs used their first names as well in their documents, but to differentiate themselves from their predecessors, they used ordinal numbers after their names. In some countries it was also common to accord "speaking" names referring to the monarch's personal traits. In France, Philip III became Philip the Bold, and the history of Denmark even knows of a Harald Bluetooth.

The same methods were used in Wallachia to differentiate between the principality's often changing princes, but the terminology was rather confusing. Princes were sometimes numbered and at other times referred to by speaking names; and their first names can also be a source of confusion, since prince Vladislav II, for example, in some documents, is also called by the name Vlad.

The epithet Dracul was first embraced by Vlad II (Vlad the Impaler's father), prince of Wallachia, after he joined the Order of the Dragon. The title could be interpreted in at least two different ways. One of the easiest explanations is that it derives from the Latin word for dragon. The Latin name for the Order of the Dragon was *Societas Draconi-*

starum. Thus, the epithet perhaps referred to the fact that Vlad II was a member of the order, and carried the meaning "one with the dragon." Another version, which has its champions among historians, is that the expression meant devil, rather than dragon. The word drac in fact means *devil* in Romanian, and the suffix -ul has the grammatical function of a definite article. *Dracul* therefore means "the devil," both in old and present-day Romanian. The epithet might have been accorded to Vlad II in reference to his shrewd double-dealing with the Hungarians and the Turks. Supporters of the dragon explanation, however, counter that the word "drac" had several meanings in old Romanian, including devil, but also dragon or demon; therefore Vlad II must have meant dragon, since he also used the motif of the dragon on his coins. These arguments might of course intertwine in a way, since the dragon was a common symbol of the devil in medieval thinking.

If we accept as fact that the epithet Dracul was originally attributed to Vlad II, we have to face the next difficult question: why does posterity link it then to his son, Vlad III? The explanation that seems the most obvious—but is not necessarily the best—is that Vlad II simply inherited the epithet from his father. The only problem with this convenient theory is that no contemporary document ever mentioned him as the son of the Dracul; rather, he gained his own well-earned epithet and was generally referred to as "Țepeș" (Impaler). The sources that referred to him as Dracul (and not just son of the Dracul) date from after his death, but they often carry contradictions and obscurities. Some claim that due to Vlad III's devilish deeds, his father's epithet was passed down to him. But this leads back to the question of whether the word originally meant dragon or devil. Popular legends depict Vlad III not only as a devilish person, but also—not long after his death—as a bloodsucking vampire, linking thus in his legendary person the name Dracula with the concept of the vampire.

COULD AN IMPALER HAVE BEEN A VAMPIRE?

Nonetheless, it is the mode of execution most favored by Vlad Țepeș III—namely, impalement—that indicates that if indeed the ruler had any knowledge of vampires, he must have been in great fear of them! After all, common wisdom considered sharpened stakes the most effective devices for disposing of vampires.

In this light, the very act of impalement would seem preventive of someone—ergo Vlad Țepeș III—transforming into a vampire. A regular rebuttal of this theory states that Vlad Țepeș could indeed still turn into a vampire, whether he was afraid of vampires in his lifetime or not.

It has also been suggested that the historical Dracula could have been Vlad IV or even V, but this theory never gained acceptance among historians or the general public. Regarding Bram Stoker's 1897 novel *Dracula*, literary critics and amateur vampire sleuths alike have had to face some problematic issues arising from the book regarding the vampire's inspiration. They finally concluded that as Stoker had limited knowledge of Transylvania, and even less regarding Wallachia, he used poetic license to conflate the figures Vlad II and III, drawing from the legends of both father and son.

Chapter 13
The Dreadful Doings of Dracula

Although we have come to no definitive resolution about the exact identity of the real-life Dracula, there can be no doubt that Vlad the Impaler formed at least a portion of the monster's personae. Yet there is considerable uncertainty about how the life and deeds of Dracula—which is to say, Vlad the Impaler—should be seen and judged. Although Wallachia played a crucial role in the defense against the Turks, it lay far away from the spiritual and political centers of Europe. Thus, little of its history seemed to be worth recording in those centers, at any rate. Most of the written sources that reveal what we know about Wallachia come, not surprisingly, from the neighboring powers that had some interest in the region, namely Hungary and Poland. As expected, only those events that held some importance to these regions were recorded, leaving much of Vlad's rule shrouded in speculation and uncertainty

A source on the character of the historical

Dracula, satirical in its tone, and most likely written in the court of Hungary's great Renaissance king, Matthias Corvinus (1443–1490), dwells at length on the sadistic inclinations of the foreign noble-man. During his captivity at Buda castle, relates the source, Dracula's favorite pastime was catching birds and mice, only to torture them to death. After methodically dismembering them, he decapitated his prey, and it is told that he killed some of the birds by plucking out their feathers one by one. After kill-ing these creatures, he never missed the opportunity to impale their bodies on his spear.

Animals are one thing, but human victims are quite another. The most dreadful doings of Drac-ula began in 1456, when he got hold of the throne of Wallachia. The available sources often depict Vlad perfecting his favorite hobby.

A SADIST'S GUIDE TO IMPALING

Impaling was one of the cruelest methods of execu-tion of Vlad's or any time. A pointed stake was intro-duced into the victim's colon, via the anus, which was then pushed up along the spinal column, if possible in a way so that no vital organs were affected, so as to prolong the victim's suffering. The stake was then made to come out between the neck and the shoulder

Engraving from book published c. 1596

blades, after which it was stuck into the ground, erecting the impaled as living monument to sadism. Sometimes the sufferings of the victim were extended by placing a "seat" on the stake, to keep the body from slipping down by its own weight. In addition to this common method of impaling, Dracula developed some new modifications for his own pleasure. For instance, he had the unfortunate victim tied to his horse and the stake introduced into his body in such a way that it impaled him as he was dragged behind the horse. Sometimes he ordered that the point of the stake should be dulled, so it would penetrate the body more slowly. In some cases the stake was driven through the victims' chests or bellies, and sometimes several victims were strung on the same stake like lines of popcorn. Some descriptions relate victims being lowered onto already erected stakes by rope, and the poor souls being impaled slowly and gradually by their own weight, suffering for as long as several days until they breathed their last. At these mass executions the stakes were arranged in geometrical patterns, often forming concentric rings. The length of the stake depended on the origins of the executed: the more distinguished the victim, the higher the stake, so it could be seen from a distance. Decomposing bodies, often left hanging on their stakes for months, filled the air with a foul smell.

MUCH AT STAKE

According to legend, Sultan Mehmed II, who gained fame by conquering Constantinople in 1453, set out to reconquer Wallachia but was stopped dead in his tracks by a horrible scene. As he marched his forces toward the bank of the river Danube, the sight of twenty thousand impaled cadavers met his gaze. The view proved so terrible that the sultan turned his troops around and called off the whole campaign.

Dracula also made incursions into southern Transylvania and impaled thousands there as a form of intimidation. According to (grossly) exaggerated figures, Dracula had ten thousand residents of Sibiu impaled and treated thirty thousand in Brașov likewise to his favorite pastime. One contemporary woodcut depicting the Brașov massacre shows Dracula holding a feast amid the impaled but still living victims. The source also mentions that Vlad Dracul, voivode of Wallachia, ate heartily while savoring the whimpering sounds of his impaled victims.

According to these descriptions, Dracula's sadistic arsenal of instruments of torture and execution were virtually limitless. Some victims were put to death by hammering a long nail into their heads, while others had their arms and legs chopped off while still alive. The latter practice was especially applied to women. Yet others were skinned alive or scalped and fed to starving wild animals; or, for variety, boiled alive. No one—regardless of rank or stature—was safe from him. He had boyars, merchants, and peasants of every age and sex impaled. Children were often pinned to their mother's breast with a stake.

VLAD'S MOTIVES

One much repeated question is what Dracula's motives—sadism aside—were for these ruthless acts of cruelty.

Some historians put his deeds down to patriotism, or otherwise try to validate his crimes through the political necessities of the time. These explanations are backed up by reports that, not long after his death, large sectors of the Wallachian population celebrated him as a national hero and protector of the Christian faith. Examples of his patriotism abound, like when a delegation of the Turkish court neglected to remove their turbans in his presence, whereby he ordered that they be nailed to the emissaries' skulls. Dracula fought several successful battles against the Turks and had every last prisoner of war impaled. He tried to justify his brutal treatment of Wallachian and Transylvanian merchants by claiming these tradesmen were originally Saxons—foreigners who had gained their riches by leeching off the local Romanian and Hungarian populations.

Others saw personal vengeance as the hidden motivator, claiming that during their Transylvanian sojourn, Dracula's family was victim of discrimination at his place of birth, the Saxon town of Sighișoara. Dracula's massacres among the Wallachian boyars are often explained as such: Wallachian nobility were voivode electors who were often disloyal to their ruler and were therefore a liability. Also, it was undoubtedly in the back of Vlad the Impaler's mind during these sessions of bloodlust how both his grandfather Mircea the Elder and his father Vlad II had been murdered through boyar conspiracies. In light of these circumstances, it became generally perceived that his treatment of the boyars was motivated by the desire to consolidate and centralize his power, as well as by personal revenge. Thus, many researchers repudiate that he found delight in the killings.

One famous story passed down from Vlad III's Wallachian reign finds Dracula holding an Easter feast in his capital, Târgoviște, to which all boyars and their families were invited. Dracula lived in constant fear of a boyar conspiracy, and suffered—as the previously mentioned circumstances suggest—from delusional paranoia. As his esteemed guests gathered for the feast, the suspicious ruler asked the assembled boyars how many voivodes had ruled them during their lifetime. The unsuspecting boyars started their count, and it was soon decided that not one of them had lived under less than seven voivodes, but some of the eldest had seen thirty rulers pass on. Dracula promptly had them all seized by his soldiers, and the elder boyars and their families were impaled on the spot. The younger boyars and their families were banished to the northern stretches of the river Argeș, where the former stronghold of the Wallachian voivodes lay in ruins. The merciless ruler had them rebuild the ancient fortress under extremely harsh conditions. Most lost their lives in the process. As far as the story can be reconstructed, Dracula systematically eliminated the old boyar families and replaced them with loyal nobility. This narrative can also be used to couch his acts of brutality as a means of stabilizing a centralized state power.

THE MORAL SADIST

Dracula had a uniquely strict moral code that he imposed upon the Wallachian people. One of its main pillars was the demand of loyalty and honesty from every member of society. Those of his subjects whose loyalty or honesty he considered dubious were promptly impaled. Another of his fundamental morals demanded an unconditional respect for property. He did not differentiate between fraudulent vendors, thieves, robbers, or looters. They all got the same punishment: impalement. A third element of Dracula's personal morality was demanding that every woman and girl live an immaculately virtuous life. His brutality targeted girls who had lost their virginity, women who committed adultery, and even disgraced widows. One account relates how Dracula convicted a woman of adultery and had her mutilated, both breasts cut off, then skinned alive and impaled on the main square of Târgoviște, while the woman's hide was displayed on a tabletop beside her.

Most of the documentation of Dracula's atrocities was recorded after his death; the earliest records were brought into circulation in Austria. It follows that some historians consider these dispatches fraudulent and consider it probable that Hungarian king Matthias Corvinus ordered their dissemination in order to justify his prolonged incarceration of Dracula. Contrary to this somewhat more sophisticated historical narrative, however, is the corpus of stories and anecdotes pervading the Balkans that are utterly irredeemable in political or moral terms. One such story is of Dracula's invitation to the impoverished, handicapped, afflicted, and vagrant subjects living in his capital for a charitable feast. Having fed them all, he suddenly bolted the doors to the banqueting hall and set the building ablaze. All his dinner guests were of course killed in the fire. A similar story relates how Dracula rounded up three hundred gypsies and had three of them grilled, then forced the others to eat the roast flesh.

Although many now claim that Dracula had always been considered a national hero in Wallachia, it was in his very homeland that a noteworthy legend sprung up about his death. The story goes that he was so despised by his people that his corpse was torn to shreds before they put him into his coffin. The coffin was later found to be completely empty. This legend clearly links Dracula's person to vampire mythology. This belief was later supplemented with stories of Dracula drinking his victims' blood and feeding on their flesh.

Chapter 14

Elizabeth Báthory:
A Female Dracula

Elizabeth (Hungarian: Erzsébet) Báthory, born in 1560 to an aristocratic Hungarian family, is one of the most famous figures in vampire lore, having gained worldwide fame, or notoriety, as a mass murderer with a distorted soul, organizer and main participant of lesbian orgies, a host of cannibalistic feasts, and someone who bathed regularly in the blood of young women to aid in the preservation of her own skin's youthful beauty. In other words: Miss Vampire 1560. The writings about her, which appear from the eighteenth century, and if gathered could probably make up a sizable library, range like a portfolio of sadistic pornography. It is not surprising that she has been depicted, in the twentieth century, in a number of horror and pornographic movies. The veracity of the horrific acts attributed to Elizabeth Báthory are, however, highly questionable and to the present day unproven.

Elizabeth Báthory was a scion of one of the most distinguished families of Hungary and Transylvania. Her parents being György Báthory and Anna Báthory, she was the offspring of a marriage between distant family members. It has been speculated that this blood marriage is the root of her supposedly troubled mind. One of her relatives was István Báthory, a maternal uncle, who in 1572 was elected reigning prince of Transylvania, and in 1576 King of Poland. She was only two when she was promised in marriage to Ferenc Nádasdy. The formal engagement was held in 1572; the wedding itself in 1575, when Báthory was but fourteen years old.

Elizabeth Báthory's husband was among the most important military leaders of a fifteen-year war with the Ottoman Turks. His courage in battle and his firm character earned him the nickname "Strong Black Bey." Since he was often away on the battlefield, however, the management of his large estates was left to Elizabeth. She did this mostly from the castle of Sárvár, which was a sort of family seat, though she also liked to stay at the castle of Csejte (Čachtice in Slovak, Schächtitz in German), which was part of the fortune she brought to the marriage. From their marriage five children were born, four of whom—Anna, Orsolya, Kata, and Pál—were still alive at the death of their father in 1604. Elizabeth

Báthory was at the time a well-respected noble-woman of Hungary, although somewhat reserved and solitary by nature. A contemporary portrait shows her as a plain-looking, withdrawn woman. No credible source gives evidence of her display-ing any stress or personality disorder during thirty years of marriage. Her husband's death burdened her with the management of the country's largest estate, along with the task of raising her children. Con-stant warfare with the Turks not only hindered her management duties, but the maintenance of military personnel to protect her castles imposed consider-able financial strain on the widow.

The widowed Elizabeth Báthory lived a notably quiet life between 1604 and 1610. Her first daughter to marry was Anna, who was betrothed to Count Miklós Zrínyi (1580–1625), followed by her daughter Kata, who was married to György Homon-nay Drugeth (1580–1620) in January 1610. Before the latter marriage, in 1609, a young nobleman named László Bende allegedly eloped with Eliza-beth Báthory, who was forty-nine at the time, in order to marry her. If this were a true story, then this László Bende most probably lusted after the wom-an's immeasurable wealth. However it happened, it seems certain enough that Elizabeth Báthory's greedy relatives soon undermined that union. Per-haps this incident was the very reason they wanted her out of the way as soon as possible, but in any case, no reliable data had come to light reporting any of the abominable atrocities she was subsequently accused of in December 1610.

THE BLOOD COUNTESS ACCUSED

One possible explanation for the character assassination of Elizabeth Báthory was the fact that she kept contact with conspicuously few people since her husband's death and boldly neglected the social obligations demanded by her status. Cloistering herself in her Csejte Castle made her person all the more intriguing for her peers and prompted what came to be the main motif of her legend: the widow shrouded in mystery. The first stories concerned with Báthory recounted the serial disappearance of

the servants and maids of Csejte Castle. These yarns, however, fail to mention any maidens by name, just as later legal proceedings neglect to name any of the alleged victims.

After rumors of Báthory's alleged

Elizabeth Báthory (1560-1514)

activity reached the royal court in Vienna, Palatine György Thurzó (1567–1616) and his men-at-arms confronted Elizabeth Báthory as she was dining in Csejte Castle on December 29, 1610, and accused her of the brutal torture, mutilation, and murder of more than six hundred innocent servants and maids and took her into custody. Allegedly, both of Elizabeth Báthory's sons-in-law participated in the raid, but there is no data to confirm that Miklós Zrínyi had actually been present at his mother-in-law's arrest. György Thurzó himself reported discovering not only a servant maid named Duricza in the throes of death by torture, but also a fully equipped torture chamber in the castle dungeon, as well as the mutilated corpses of murdered maidens in the house of horrors, Csejte Castle.

Palatine Thurzó conducted the interlocutory legal proceedings against Elizabeth Báthory with commendable expediency in January 1611without the consent of Hungarian king Matthias II (1557–1619). Four of her handmaids were interrogated under torture and thereby no doubt testified to things they couldn't have seen in their worst nightmares. Báthory appealed in vain for a fair trial procedure appropriate to her rank, and with due deference to her own testimony, the woman was accused of mass murder without a single hearing. Thurzó declared her guilty of having had "a large number of innocent maidens, noble and common handmaids ... put to death without legal process, having horribly and utterly murdered them, mutilated their bodies, and burned them with red hot irons, torn and roasted their flesh, forcing them to eat the cooked pieces."

As partners in crime, the handmaids testifying under torture were promptly executed, and Bathory was sentenced to lifelong entombment in a windowless chamber of the Csejte Castle. Though Matthias II made repeated demands for a retrial, György Thurzó disobeyed the king's order on account of the key witnesses having already been executed. The legality and credibility of the whole ordeal was highly dubious, and the obvious question arises: whose interest was best served by the conviction of Elizabeth Báthory? She had already decided to divide her immense fortune between her descendants, and suspicion thus falls squarely on her new son-in-law, György Homonnay Drugeth and those who wanted to hastily acquire her wealth. György Thurzó's likely motive might have been an ambitious palatine's attempt to vanquish Elizabeth's nephew, Gábor Báthory, Prince of Transylvania (1589–1613), who was aspiring to the Hungarian throne. Thurzó was quite obviously aiming for Gábor Báthory's princedom, even going as far as organizing a (failed) murder plot against the prince in 1610, finding a fellow conspirator in Homonnay Drugeth.

Depicting Elizabeth Báthory as a sadistic murderer came in handy for her prosecutors on several counts. For one, the accusation was a serious blow to the throne-aspiring Báthory family's credibility, while at the same time the relatives got their inheritance before Elizabeth might have considered remarrying. This was likely the reason Elizabeth wasn't charged with treason or conspiracy along with her nephew Gábor Báthory; for the law would have required capital punishment and a full confiscation of property. Elizabeth Báthory was kept locked away in the Csejte Castle for four years, and the harsh treatment soon led to the deterioration of her health. Throughout the four years she refused to admit to any of the crimes of which she had been convicted. Tormented to the utmost, the wretched woman took the formal step of making her bequest early in 1614 and conspicuously left most of her fortune to son-in-law Homonnay Drugeth rather than her own son. Then she died suddenly. Her death is reported thus in the diaries of one of Thurzó's underlings: "Incarcerated she was indefinitely for her horrific and unspeakable deeds of four years before, and it was there in Csejte that she breathed her last."

ELIZABETH BÁTHORY DIES,
AND A LEGEND IS BORN

Despite a complete lack of legitimate evidence, Elizabeth Báthory's reputation as the "Blood Countess" grew in stature and she became a diabolical symbol of human ruthlessness and cruelty. Most frequently, she is accused of bathing in the blood of her servants. Certain versions of this legendary bloodbath convey the notion that by bathing in the blood of cruelly tortured and murdered young virgins, Countess Báthory undertook to preserve her own youth and beauty. The logic behind the legend is flawed, as Elizabeth Báthory had not been especially beautiful in her youth. Even so, these most probably fabricated horrific acts were often attributed to her sexual aberrations. According to these accounts, the heinous murders were acts of sacrifice on the altar of erotic attractiveness and female vanity; that is to say, the sight of agony and death were supposedly a sort of spiritual and sexual climax for Elizabeth Báthory.

Bathing in blood is a ritual with roots among ancient peoples, as evident in their myths. It was distinguished early on from the ritual anointment of blood, which had sacred meaning in some cultures and was retained as a ritual until quite recent times. In contrast with the latter, it can be considered a sort of offshoot of the age-old practice of cannibalism. It is no coincidence that the charges against Báthory included this crime. Selected virgins were mutilated, it was claimed; tongs were used to tear chunks of their living flesh from their bodies and the morsels cooked. The victims were forced to eat their own flesh as well as each other's, and the Countess also helped herself with a hearty appetite.

While few historians lend credence to the veracity of the Blood Countess's crimes, her name will forever be tied to bloodlust and vampirism due to her historical and physical proximity to Vlad the Impaler—and, frankly, the lies created about her person are far more interesting than the bland truth.

Csejte Castle, Elizabeth Báthory's home—and prison

Chapter 15

Tainted Blood

The basic premise of vampire mythology is that sucking blood from a healthy, living human is necessary to revitalize the vampire. Blood has been revered as an essential part of our life force since prehistoric times; both quantity (full-bloodedness) and consistency were both regarded as vitally significant. Hence the portrayal of vampires with pale, waxy complexions suggested that their bodies lacked a sufficient natural supply of blood. For vampires, blood is a source of nutrition, which must be continuously replenished. The legend is based on earlier myths, partly those alluding to the sacred ritual of anointment with blood, and the portrayal of bathing in blood. A third element is the motif of incest. Certain communities emerging from a matriarchal structure soon recognized that sexual congress between close relatives often produced degenerate offspring, which was deemed a violation of family blood, or consanguineal incest. Not all societies barred this practice;

the pharaohs of ancient Egypt for instance preferred marriage among their blood relations, in order to better preserve their sacred bloodline. Pharaohs were commonly married to their own sisters, nieces, or adolescent daughters.

Christianity and the Roman Catholic Church not only considered incest an aberration, but a major, deadly sin, and explicitly forbade marriage or sexual acts among close relations. In medieval Christian states, violators of this restriction faced serious consequences, often in the form of a death sentence. However, under special political terms, the Holy See would permit certain monarchs to join with their relatives in matrimony. Thus it was common practice, for example, for members of the Habsburg dynasty to marry cousins or second cousins, which primarily served to preserve and expand the family's wealth and power. Incest was nevertheless a sin for monarchs, too, and popes made routine use of this fact in achieving their political aims, as monarchs living in a sinful liaison were subject to blackmail, the threat of their marriages being declared illegal and void, and their offspring declared illegitimate.

THE BÁTHORY LINEAGE

The most infamous incest case in Hungarian history

is connected to the aforementioned, doomed Báthory family. The accused were in this case none other than Elizabeth Báthory's nephew Gábor Báthory and his sister Anna. But who was this family, with three of its members accused of the worst crimes imaginable? We're talking about one of the most significant noble families in Transylvania, which rose to prominence from the ancient Hungarian Gutkeled clan. During the reign of Charles I of Hungary, this family acquired estates in two counties, Ecsed and Kraszna. Not long after, the Báthory family split into two branches, and of these, the Ecsed branch soon gained national prominence. After Hungary itself was split into two, then three parts, members of the Ecsed line supported the Habsburgs, while the other, Somlyó line, backed the Szapolyai family. This latter leaning also implied a pro-Turkish orientation. János Zsigmond Szapolyai I, Prince of Transylvania, appointed István Báthory of the Somlyó branch the ruler of Oradea (Hungarian: Nagyvárad; German: Grosswardein), and he was in turn elected Prince of Transylvania after János Zsigmond's death. In 1576, he was also elected King of Poland. As István Báthory was without an heir, he appointed Zsigmond, the son of Kristóf Báthory, heir to the princely throne. Another nephew by the name of István was appointed Lord of Oradea, a seat of key strategic significance at the time. The latter nephew sired a son in Oradea, Gábor Báthory, who was born in 1589 and was the last in line to bear the title of Prince of Transylvania, from 1608 to 1613.

Gábor Báthory was taken into the court of Transylvanian prince István Bocskai (1557–1606) and was appointed the prince's heir at the age of sixteen. However, nobles backing the Habsburg dynasty wanted to impede another Báthory's princedom. They succeeded in the short term, for Zsigmond Rákóczi (1595–1620) was named Prince of Transylvania. Gábor Báthory, however, found new allies from the ranks of the Hajduk and Szekler populations and managed to convince Zsigmond Rákóczi to renounce his title. Báthory's basic aim was to subdue the Romanian principalities, acquire the Polish throne, and banish the Habsburgs from the Kingdom of Hungary, thereby creating a strong empire under his own rule, albeit one ostensibly paying allegiance to the Turks. Under the prevailing political climate, these aims were utterly unrealistic, though his political maneuvering had proved initially successful.

In the Kingdom of Hungary, Báthory's main rival was Palatine György Thurzó, who would attempt to extend his monstrous accusations beyond just Elizabeth Báthory to implicate the entire Báthory family. It was no wonder that gossip soon arose of the youthful, strong, and handsome Gábor Báthory's "hot-bloodedness"—a trait that, it was alleged, led him to defile women of virtue, rape any who dared resist, and even enter into an incestuous relationship with his own sister, Anna. Anna was age eight at the time the charge of "incestuous lubricity" was brought against her, topped with the preposterous claim that she was engaged in a lesbian relationship with her aunt, the Blood Countess herself. Alongside these allegations, numerous attempts were made to unseat Gábor Báthory, including several conspiracies both in Transylvania and Hungary, until one finally succeeded when the prince was murdered in 1613 in Oradea.

What remains obscured is the role Gábor Báthory's successor, Transylvanian prince Gábor Bethlen (1580–1629), might have played in his murder, given that Bethlen most benefited from the act. Bethlen himself was a strong proponent of the charges against Gábor Báthory and went on to instigate a witch trial against Anna, whom he termed the "Devil's murderous whore" in one of his letters. Born in 1594, Anna Báthory was married off to Dénes Bánffi at the age of twelve. Bánffi was a close relative of the renowned Transylvanian nobleman István Bocskai. Anna became a widow by the age of sixteen and entered her second marriage that same year with Zsigmond Jósika, a boy her age. That very year, she was accused of leading a lewd and immoral life and bearing an illegitimate child from one János Kra-

jnik. Her husband defended her from these allegations by acknowledging the child as his own, but the
accusers quickly changed tack and charged her and
two female relations with witchcraft. At one point,
prince Gábor Bethlen sentenced her and her two
female relatives to beheading and confiscation of all
their property, but Anna was granted a pardon.

The unlucky Anna Báthory retreated to her
estate in Kereki, only to be tried as a witch again in
1618. During those court proceedings she was once
more charged with incest and sexual aberrations.
These charges of moral corruption and debauchery
were backed up vehemently by the earlier allegations
of Anna's incestuous relationship with her brother
and her consequently tainted blood. The woman
was finally placed under custody. Her only means
to gain freedom was to "voluntarily" donate a large
portion of her estates and all her gold and silverware
to her accuser, Prince Gábor Bethlen.

In 1621, her third witch trial was initiated,
and during this ordeal Anna was even accused of
murdering her own son, who was alive and in good
health in the Kingdom of Hungary at the time. The
incest charge was now augmented with a blood libel
charge—that is, of sacrificing her child's blood for
her dark practices. Anna Báthory was allowed to live
also after this third trial, but her castle in Ecsed, as
well as its grounds and her estate in Tășnad (Tasnád

in Hungarian; Trestenburg in German), were seized by the Bethlen family. The dispossessed woman fled to her relatives in Poland. There she lived in considerable misery and opted to return to Hungary in 1636, appealing to palatine Miklós Esterházy for assistance, and was granted a modest pension. She visited Transylvania in 1640 in an attempt to reappropriate some of her confiscated property. She was detained in Târgu Mureş (Hungarian: Marosvásárhely; German: Neumarkt) and subjected to yet another witch trial, her fourth. Although she was allowed once again to go free, the unfortunate woman thenceforth passed from view of our sources.

In many a twentieth-century vampire story, when a vampire creates another vampire by coercing a human to drink of its blood, this act is known as a blood bond. Blood bonds are a strong tie between the vampire and its new offspring, itself now a vampire, and cement the vampire's mystic power over the underling. In these stories, blood bonds between vampires can be considered analogous with incest between humans. In this mythic connection, incest is a supernatural union of two blood relations, whereby they partake of special, unearthly powers, and as we can see, such superstitions can lead to tragic ends for those accused of this moral crime.

Chapter 16

A French Dracula

Gilles de Rais, who lived in France during the era of the Hundred Years' War (1337–1453), was a contemporary of Vlad Țepeș, the famed Dracula from Wallachia. Some of the terrible crimes he was accused of, however, recall those that Elizabeth Báthory was convicted of some two hundred years later. These similarities are noteworthy, since his life and reputation had an effect on the formation of the vampire legend, just as his Eastern European counterparts did. Likewise with other "real life" vampires, the question is if he really committed some of the crimes he was accused of. Finding a well-founded answer to this question from such a distance in time is rather difficult.

Gilles de Rais, born in 1404, was a scion of

one of the most ancient and distinguished families of Brittany. At the age of eleven he became an orphan, and from then his upbringing was left to his maternal grandfather, Jean de Craon. In 1420, the sixteen-year-old Gilles de Rais, with the consent of his grandfather, abducted and married his first cousin, Catherine de Thouras, who was heiress to a vast fortune. Not much later the recently widowed Jean de Craon led to the altar the grandmother of Gilles's new wife. From this point on grandson and grandfather made it a joint project to trick their new relations out of their fortune. They went as far as subduing Catherine, sewing her into a sack, throwing her into the river, and not coming to her aid unless she signed over all of her inheritance to them.

GILLES DE RAIS AND JOAN OF ARC

In this era the French throne was occupied by Charles VI (the Beloved, the Mad), who was unable to maintain strong royal power and did not take sufficient steps to repel renewed militaristic attacks by the English. Some French nobles took advantage of the relative anarchy to supplement their fortunes by robbing, intimidating, and using all forms of violence against their victims. Charon and his grandson de Rais were two among these nobles.

Gilles de Rais (1404-1440)

I n 1429 Gilles de Rais lent his own troops, at his own expense, to the campaign led by the peasant girl Joan of Arc (the Virgin of Orléans) against the English invaders. He played an important role in her victory near Orléans, and the twenty-five-year-old nobleman was promoted to the rank of Marshall by the new King of France, Charles VII. Not much later, Joan of Arc fell into captivity and was sentenced by the British to burn at the stake. Some have claimed that de Rais tried freeing her by armed attack, but no credible sources verify this.

After his grandfather, Jean de Craon, died in 1432, Gilles de Rais retired from the royal court. Back at his estates in Brittany, he began cultivating the appearance of an upstanding citizen, focusing his attention on religious ceremonies. He generously supported church choirs and spent large sums to stage spectacular plays. His lavish spending met with the increasing apprehension of his family, and was indeed rationalized by his supposed madness, in a posthumous biography. Furthermore, his younger brother and nephews persuaded King Charles VII, in 1453, to forbid him from selling any of his estates. Despite the warning, Gilles de Rais went on squandering his wealth to the point where he was all but impoverished. This in turn led to his new passion—alchemy. He believed with increasing fervor that this pseudoscience would allow him to produce large quantities of gold. He undertook burdensome expenses to set up a well-appointed laboratory, distressing his family to the point where they actually took up arms and occupied his two castles to prevent him from pawning them off.

GILLES DE RAIS STANDS ACCUSED

In 1440 Gilles de Rais, his fortune spent, made an attempt to reconquer one of his castles. By that time, the castle had been placed under the stewardship of the Catholic Church. Due to this reckless action, the bishop of Nantes led an investigation against de Rais for breaching the Holy Church. This trial soon took an entirely new direction with the inclusion of several new charges, according to which Gilles de

Rais had fallen into the sin of heresy, using arcane practices to summon supernatural powers, including demons, and moreover leveling against him the charge of sodomy and homosexuality, including the corruption and murder of young boys.

Thus the onetime national hero, scourge of the English, had been transformed in the public eye into a homosexual pedophile and a sadistic murderer who also happened to be Satan's emissary on Earth. Due to the gravity of these charges, John V, Prince of Brittany, had Gilles de Rais arrested immediately together with four of his men who were accused of being accomplices to murder.

The inquisitor assigned by the Catholic Church summed up the charges against Gilles de Rais in forty-nine points. Initially, de Rais denied all charges and refused to acknowledge the inquisitor's authority. Later, however, quite unaccountably, he recognized the court and admitted to most of the charges, except for summoning the devil, which he denied. During the proceedings, de Rais and his accomplices were charged with the murder of almost 140 children, young boys for the most part, for use in their satanic practices. According to the inquest, de Rais engaged in fornication with the boys, whom he murdered himself or had murdered. The most horrifying accounts report that he often satisfied his sexual urges on the bodies of the dying children. The inquest describes cases where de Rais hung children, only to release them again before they were finally suffocated. He allegedly repeated this "game" with several of his little victims, before having one of his henchmen slash the poor child's throat. He then had the beheaded youngsters' corpses disemboweled, and gazed with relish upon their internal organs. Allegedly, the murdered children were finally burned, and their ashes scattered into a nearby river. Further charges accused de Rais of even more serious crimes, as listed in the inquest. These included engaging in occult magical practices, summoning the dead, and offering the dead children's hands, eyes, and hearts to the devil, in order to commune with Satan.

Testimonies recorded during the trial list thirty-five boys by name who had disappeared near de Rais's castle, even though there was no evidence apart from hearsay to prove they were actually murdered by de Rais or his servants. As there was no substantial evidence, the justices decided to subject de Rais to torture. De Rais opted to confess to avoid torture, and "voluntarily" admitted to the charges brought against him. After his confession, the Church court passed the case on to the secular court, which pronounced him guilty of heresy, sodomy, and devil worship. He was then excommunicated from the church, and sentenced to death by hanging, after which his corpse was to be burned at the stake. Due to his repentant behavior, however, he was received back into communion with the Church even if he was not to escape with his life. Two of his convicted accomplices were executed alongside him. His accusers believed that the fire that consumed his already hanged body ultimately cleansed de Rais of his sin, freeing him from the clutches of Satan.

Today, most French historians refute that de Rais committed the inhuman horrors he was convicted of, and support the position that the prince of Brittany and the bishop of Nantes joined forces to eliminate the increasingly bothersome nobleman. It is certain that convicting de Rais was in their foremost interests, as it was the only way they could hang on to his entitled—and thus theoretically revocable—castle properties. In any case, the legend of Gilles de Rais was kept alive for centuries in France. Folklore connected devil worship and summoning with the legend of resurrecting the dead, and thereby entered de Rais into the canon of vampire mythology.

Chapter 17
The Vampiress of Venice

While plenty of written records have survived from the Middle Ages attesting to vampire myths, hardly any physical evidence beyond that has remained to lend such words credibility. That is why a discovery by University of Florence anthropologist Matteo Borrini, based on research and excavations he conducted in 2006 and 2007 near Venice, related to an outbreak of the plague in 1576, created a sensation among both the public and scholars alike.

Notwithstanding its relatively small size, Venice had by the twelfth century become a major trading and naval power of the Mediterranean region. A century later it was one of the richest and most influential of all city-states in Europe. Built on swampy islands in the largest lagoon in the Adriatic Sea, Venice may have been well defended against attack from the mainland, but the diseases brought home by sailors and others by sea left it vulnerable indeed.

Spread by a bacteria, usually as the result of a bite by an infected flea (*xenopsylla cheopis*; the rat flea), bubonic plague killed some 25 million people in fourteenth-century Europe and millions more in smaller outbreaks in the centuries to follow. The bacteria becomes localized in an infected lymph node—usually in the groin, armpits; before long, the immune system collapses and the lack of oxygen in the most severely affected areas of the skin yields black, necrotized tissue: hence the disease's common name, "Black Death."

To defend against the plague, Venice imposed the world's first major quarantine on the island of Lazzaretto Nuovo in 1468: every arriving ship had to wait in port for at least a week to ensure the city authorities that no infected persons would be getting off. Thanks to this policy, Venice did prove more resistant to the plague than did many other reaches of Europe. But its efforts did not always prove successful.

The year 1576 saw yet another plague outbreak ravage Venice. As earlier, the dead were buried in a mass grave on Lazzaretto Nuovo. It was in excavating this grave more than four centuries later that Matteo Borrini and his team of researchers happened upon the earthly remains of that woman who, after her death, apparently had a brick stuffed into her mouth—with such force that some of her teeth broke off in the process.

According to some contemporary myths, vampires were responsible for such epidemics. More specifically, it was believed that vampires that had unwittingly been buried alongside plague victims, and that once there, these representatives of the undead took the welcome opportunity to gorge themselves on the flesh—and, yes, the blood—of the innocents nestled up so close. Once sated and revived, the vampires would climb out off their graves, and again attack the living, spreading the disease as they went, and thus prolonging the epidemic. Gravediggers were responsible for identifying the vampires among the dead. Upon thorough examination, corpses suspected of being vampires had bricks stuffed into their mouths to render them incapable of more feasting, leaving them forever powerless underground.

As determined by modern-day researchers, the linking of vampire myths with plague outbreaks

occurred because, in fact, blood often flowed from the mouths of plague victims—at times soaking right through their burial shrouds until, over time, the shrouds themselves seemed to have been ripped apart by teeth. In contract with classic Dracula myths, such vampires specialized not only in the drinking of blood, but in chewing away at the shrouds and the flesh of those nearby. Those suspected of such vampiric behavior in mass graves were almost exclusively women—just why, remains a mystery. The skeleton excavated in Venice and then examined with the methods of modern anthropology, in any case, proved to be from a woman of about sixty years old—old for that era.

In announcing his discovery at a session of the American Academy of Forensic Science in Denver, Colorado, Borrini noted that this might well have been the first instance of a vampire having undergone forensic examination. His announcement stirred debate. Said Wichita State University researcher Peer Moore-Jansen, "While Borrini's finding is exciting, claiming it as the first vampire is a little ridiculous." Moore-Jansen, who reported having found similar skeletons in Poland, interpreted Borrini's work more as the first archaeological evidence of vampire hunting. In his reply, Borrini further clarified his own conclusions to say he believed this grave to represent the first instance of archeological proof of a physical defense against evil.

Part III
Bad Beings, Distant (Undead) Relatives, and More

Chapter 18

Demons

No discussion of vampires can be complete without at least a brief look back to the popular notions of Evil (with a capital "E") that, together with so many other factors rooted in both the fine details and the broad brushstrokes of history, helped shape these monsters in the human imagination to begin with. As the biblical Satan (Hebrew: *ha-Satan*, or "the opposer")—appointed by God to test man's faith? fallen angel out to get God?—and Lucifer (Hebrew: *hēlēl*, or "shining one") became synonymous with the Devil among Christians across Europe and beyond, and as both morphed into so many other guises over the centuries—including demons, of course—it seems reasonable to start out by helping ourselves to just a bite off demonology.

Judeo-Christian conceptions of beings with terrifying supernatural powers can be traced back, in no small part, to a rich body of traditions whose recorded roots stretch back to the mythology of the ancient world, Egypt and Greece in particular. The word "demon" itself derives from the Greek term *daimon*, which was used to refer to good or benevolent nature spirits that could influence human character and behavior. Later, however, the concept took on increasingly negative associations, with the Judeo-Christian "demon" referring to malevolent spirits only. In the world of the imagination and folklore demons were to become beings that bring trouble, sorrow, and misery to humankind. The superior powers they possessed enabled them to keep their chosen victims under their influence, make them servants deprived of their own free will, and even provoke them to commit evil deeds.

Since demons were originally imagined as immaterial, disembodied forces, physical traits were not attributed to them. This did not mean, however, that they were imperceptible. The appearance of a demon was occasionally said, for example, to be accompanied by sound and light disturbances such as a sudden breeze or an indistinct shadow. Some demons could appear in a physical, material form as well. This could happen in such a way that the demon entered the body of some earthly entity (including animals, humans, weather phenomena), or on other occasions it created a body for itself, a monster on earth.

Jewish folklore classified demons unequivocally as negative beings that tempted individuals to betray their religion and their alliance with God. Fear of demons and protection against them was indeed a community-building force. Jews used various names for assorted demons. Satan was the evil force that opposes religion; Belial was the spirit of perversion, wickedness, and annihilation; while Mastema was an angel that persecuted evil on behalf of God, who permitted him to have demons as his subordinates.

Christianity viewed demons as fallen angels

Christ and the Devil (ancient bas relief, Pisa, Italy)

that employed their keen intelligence to indulge in their diabolical activities. Through the Middle Ages demons were increasingly associated with the Seven Deadly Sins, and complex hierarchic systems were set up to classify them. By the Reformation, in the sixteenth century, demons were, roughly speaking, classified as follows:

- Lucifer: pride
- Mammon: avarice
- Azmodeus: lust
- Satan: wrath
- Beelzebub: gluttony
- Leviathan: envy
- Belfegor: sloth

The belief in demons was common throughout the Medieval Ages, handed down to us through tales and legends. Magic practices were exercised to control these unwanted guests. Magic words—incantations and prayers—were muttered in the hope of keeping the evil away. But sometimes the magic of words was used with ill intentions—namely, to bring evil forces upon an enemy by showering him with curses.

Popular belief held that demons could move between Earth and the world beyond. Many stories illustrate that if a coffin was left open, and a black cat jumped it over, or a bat or an owl flew above, an evil being would possess these creatures. In some super-stitions black cats, bats, and owls are seen as possible physical manifestations of evil.

In the world of the popular imagination these stories drew a connection between these demonic shape-shifters and other familiar agents of evil; namely, witches, werewolves, and—our old friend—the vampire.

Chapter 19

Fairies and Witches

With roots in the most ancient mythologies, fairies and witches remain among the most common figures in the modern popular imagination.

Fairies are today often imagined as pretty, dancing, mostly benevolent female figures that can cast spells and perform magic. Typically tied to a specific geographic location—often a place appreciated by humans for its beauty or mystery, such as mountain peaks or caves, catacombs in castle ruins, or the dark depths of lakes and brooks—fairies only leave their dwelling places at certain times. After making a fleeting appearance in a form visible to humans, they return to where they belong.

But not all fairies have the best of intentions. With their gaze alone, mischievous fairies might enchant young man who, under the spell, desires only to follow the fairy, unable to escape—unless the man happens to have some supernatural abilities himself. Fairies that are downright harmful make up

a minority. These are in fact demons. These bad fairies corrupt people's souls, cast spells on them, and drive their victims into eternal physical and spiritual damnation. In Eastern European cultures, the belief in fairies was especially strong among Romanians and Hungarians. The Romanians tended to regard them as female; while as evident from Hungarian folklore, the latter imagined fairies also to be male.

In the centuries following the collapse of the Roman Empire, Christians generally did not yet consider such beings with supernatural powers a serious threat. This was in part because people who excelled in exorcism were believed to efficiently keep Satan and his evil demons away from humankind. From the eleventh century on, however, the notion of evil as a malevolent, threatening, unavoidable force had gained ground among commoners—so much so, that the Church believed its power almost rivaled that of God.

WHICH WITCH?

Severe famines, growing social inequality, and ever more frequent epidemics across Europe were all seen as the work of Satan—whom the Church and other authorities conceived of as a dangerous symbol of "natural" freedom, as a force opposing the feudal order. Satan the seditious. Any rebellion against the established social order was therefore considered the work of Satan, and crushed. Anything that stood out became suspicious, and traditional healing practices, performed mostly by women, originally a part of community life, were no exception. Over time, such suspicions gave rise to a belief in the existence of witches—a belief that gained such momentum that the Church became involved in its official prosecution, terrifying populations across Europe with a succession of witch trials and executions.

Although people have long conceived of witches as either male or female, in the popular imagination across much of the globe in recent centuries, and especially in modern times, women have been the primary suspects. The earliest beliefs recorded in the annals of European folklore included such particulars as the notion that witches are born with tails and can be recognized thus. Although they were seen as essentially human, witches were believed to possess exceptional supernatural capacities—saliently, those allowing them to cast spells and protect themselves and others against a spell or black magic. Some legends held that witches, as the female servants of Satan, taint the blood of humans through their magic. Eastern European folklore includes stories of witches killing their victims with potions that turned their blood into poison or else made blood evaporate, in which case the victims transformed into the living dead.

Indeed, the mythology surrounding witchcraft includes plenty of vampirelike behavior and blood-related rituals. Some early legends suggested that witches were humans by day, turning into spirits by night. They were regarded as being learned in ancient supernatural practices, which made it hard for common humans to outsmart them.

According to Church teachings, the best protection against a witch was prayer, but—again reminiscent of vampirism—it was likewise considered effective to pin a clove of garlic on your hat. But no ordinary clove—one that had been grown out from out a dead snake's head.

HURRY, OR WE'LL BE LATE FOR THE WITCH BURNING!

But the belief in witches sometimes passed from legend into real life. Notably, the Hungarian King Saint Stephen, who ruled from 1000 to 1038, passed laws designed to protect the general public from a scourge of witches. Among them was one that read, "No one should dare to use any witchcraft or devilish practice to make a person lose his mind and perish. If a woman endeavors to commit such practices, she shall be given into the hands of whom she had bewitched, or into the hands of that person's relatives, so that they might judge her according to their will. And if a fortuneteller is found to be using woodashes and such in their practice, the bishop should bring them to justice with a whip."

These words from the long arm of early Hungarian law reveal that the nation's first king saw witchcraft as a superstitious practice that recently Christianized people were still practicing in their ignorance, unless they had already been reeducated by a bishop's whip. A century later, witchcraft still appeared to be a serious menace if the laws of King Saint László (1077–1096) are to be taken at face value, under which "witches are to find their punishment as a bishop thinks right."

But then along came King Kálmán I (c. 1074–1116; commonly known in English as Coloman I)—who was nicknamed "Kálmán the Book Lover" because of his literacy and education. Kálmán held his predecessors' belief in witches to be superstition, and he added this into law: "As for witches, there should be no mention of any kind of them, since they don't exist."

Some medieval chroniclers assumed later that King Kálmán ordered this in self defense, believing that he was a witch himself and had been lobbied by the Devil. Despite his effort to eradicate witch-hunting, this practice continued to be fairly common in Hungary well into later centuries, and was even institutionalized—as elsewhere in Europe—under the Church.

Witch trials kept courts busy all across Medieval Europe. Since many people thought witches capable of assuming the appearance of any animal, there are detailed records of trials in which sheep, pigs, and even flies were brought to trial under an accusation of witchcraft.

The most common victims of witch hysteria outbreaks remained, however, unfortunate women of all social classes. The Church, in its efforts to hunt down witches, relied on a great numbers of judges, exorcists, torturers, executioners, and eyewitnesses drawn from common folk. The female victims were subjected to the most terrible tortures and were persuaded to admit anything simply to make their suffering end. In the course of their interrogations they were also asked to name accomplices, who were then accused in turn, so that each accusation was apt to snowball into many others.

A common myth held that burning witches at the stake had a purifying effect, and liberated them from their sins. What is more, doing so made for an altogether riveting popular attraction, and it is not too far off base to label it medieval reality TV. Sometimes up to a hundred witches went up in flames on the same day, with onlookers celebrating by feasting on good meals and buying souvenirs from vendors who has set up stalls on the spot. Mass executions were interrupted by processions, which included parades and the burning of straw puppets. All in all, the sight of witches and others being burned at the stake was a fairly common experience for centuries in medieval Europe and, in some areas, into more recent centuries.

In the world of the popular imagination— tales and legends—there was often a fluid transition between the worlds of fairies and the witches. The abilities and characteristics of the "bad" fairies are practically identical with those of witches. The main difference was that the fairies not only seemed harmless, but also proved harmless most of the time (in legend at least), while witches seemed inoffensive during the day—only to get their evil practices going full-force under the cover of night. On the other hand, if there is no evidence of burning fairies at the stake, it might be because they are so hard to catch.

Chapter 20

Golem

The next time you're at a party attended by fans of the undead or the unliving, as the case may be, and you're looking for something smart with which to break an awkward moment of silence, remember the homunculus. Latin for "little man," this term has been used for centuries in referring to the concept of a tiny, fully developed human body—whether by those who once believed that human sperms or eggs were in fact complete little people from the outset, or in referring to creatures believed to be made of lifeless material to serve the individual behind their creation. As for the latter, we're talking a category apart from the usual demons, fairies, and witches. And yet these artificial beings are surrounded by a varied collection of often hair-raising myths whose roots stretch back to ancient times. Those tales in which these creatures began acting independently of their creator's will, often perpetrating terrible acts and offences against society, became especially popular, and they still are.

The term "homunculus" was perhaps first used by the Swiss-German physician, botanist, alchemist, and astrologer Paracelsus (1493–1541), who is credited as the first systematic botanist. The *homunculus* he originally described was an artificial creature created through alchemy.

The myth of creating a human being out of blood and clay can be traced back to the earliest Sumerian legends of Mesopotamia, however. The god Enki, the "Lord of the Earth," created a human being from mud to serve him. Later Enki also created, likewise from mud, two genderless beings—Galaturra and Kurgarra—to guard water and food. He sent them down to the netherworld, where they managed to resuscitate Inanna, the goddess of fertility and warfare. These genderless beings are early archetypes of what came to be known in medieval Europe as golems.

Over the second millennium bc, the Akkadians, arriving from the center of Babylon, invaded the Sumerian city states in the southern part of Mesopotamia. The imprint of this conflict appeared in mythology in the guise of battles between old and new gods. The goddess Tiamat was of Sumerian origin, and in the war between the old and new gods, it was her son (and lover), Kingu, who commanded the army of the old gods, made up of monsters, in battle against the goddess Ea, who, of Akkadian origin, reigned over the earth and seas. But Ea was so terrified by this onslaught of monsters that he fled, whereupon his son took command of the new legion of gods and managed to overcome and kill Kingu. The son then mixed the blood of Kingu with clay, and created the first human being to serve the gods. This was Marduk, who was the manifestation of the spring sunshine; and who had four eyes and four ears, multiple tongues of fire rising from his throat, and giant hands and feet. In a tribute to his overthrow of the old gods, the new gods awarded him fifty titles, including "Great Fighter" and "Lord of Life."

Many versions of the Mesopotamian legends lived on for centuries in the teachings of several sacred writings and through the people of the Middle East, including Jews who adopted elements of these legends.

In its one biblical occurrence, in Psalms, the Hebrew word transliterated into English as *golem* meant an amorphous, shapeless substance—and as such it was passed down into medieval writing. Jewish folklore came to use the word in referring to a moving but not living being made of inanimate matter. Kabbalistic Jewish tradition chronicles several stories about great masters, famous rabbis of old who allegedly knew how to produce robotlike servants from clay mixed with human blood, using a

The Golem and Rabbi Loew ben Bezalel (© Eugene Ivanov)

sacred word of command. Written religious law was seen as being accessible to all, whereas the Kabbalah was arcane and obscure, available only to the chosen few. In its mystical world, biblical words and phrases were believed to each hold a hidden, mysterious meaning. At the core of the Kabbalah was a system of numerology, which stated that certain biblical passages comprised not only words but also numbers, which could be tallied to decode other words. By deciphering the links between words and numbers, the Kabbalah represented a unique new way of interpreting scripture.

According to Jewish legend, Rabbi Elijah Ba'al Shem (1550–1583) of Chelm, Poland, created a golem in the sixteenth century, inscribing on its forehead the secret name of God. His golem continued to grow, however, against his will, and became increasingly frightening, so the rabbi finally destroyed it by deleting the Hebrew letter Aleph from the word *emet* (truth), thereby spelling the word *mavet* (dead) on the golem's forehead—after which the monster crumbled into dust.

The best-known golem creator was however another master, Rabbi Judah Loew ben Bezalel (c. 1520–1609), who lived in Prague. Like Rabbi Elijah, he also had to destroy his monstrous creation with his own hands, after it desecrated the Holy Sabbath.

Tradition has it that Rabbi Loew was greatly troubled not only by the overall suffering of his people but also by the religious persecution they faced as Jews. He pondered how he could help. One day he remembered a childhood story he had heard of a humanoid figure formed from blood and mud, the Golem, which obeyed its master's bidding. After thorough research in the Kabbalah, the rabbi found the secret of how to create an artificial servant; and, using mud from the bank of the Vltava river, he made a golem of his own. The Golem slept by day, and by night it did everything its master commanded. Rabbi Loew wanted the Golem to resemble a human in every respect, so he taught it to read. The Golem was then able to learn the ways of humanity from books, and thus came to be discontent with its own, banal fate. Work alone held no satisfaction for it anymore—it longed to play, to have fun. One day, the creature escaped the rabbi's home. People ran from it in fright, which angered the Golem into smashing everything in its path in a fit of rage. In the end, the people of the neighborhood gathered together and chased the unfortunate Golem away.

It would be easy to see this as the inspiration for Mary Shelley's *Frankenstein*. In fact, the story of Prague's Rabbi Loew has been retold in different versions by many writers, perhaps the best known adaptation being Isaac Bashevis Singer's short story "The Golem."

Romanticism was a period with great affinity for mysticism and the sensual, and as such it reshaped the image of the golem into that of yet another example of magical evil. It took only one more, small step to eventually position the golem as a star in the modern genre of horror literature and film. This may have been linked to a notion rooted in late-nineteenth century anti-Semitism—namely, that masters of the Kabbalah had created vampires, or were vampires themselves, and that golems were the instruments of their poisonous arts. Or, more likely, the creature was just too appealing to the human imagination to let it rest. He was created to do our bidding, so why not also serve the will of horror writers and film producers alike?

Chapter 21
Voodoo and Zombies

The extent to which voodoo and zombies go hand in hand is less than straightforward, but in one Caribbean nation these traditions have long over-lapped—which is not to mention that in the popular imagination of the world at large they certainly do. And so here they are sharing a chapter that takes a look at these religious practices that have long fascinated so many in the "civilized" West and helped shape those corners of our mind where Dracula also dwells.

To the common observer, voodoo is one of the world's most impenetrable and unique religions. Its roots go back to the Kingdom of Dahomey (today Behin) and other regions of West Africa—and it was to flourish, in a form camouflaged by and later seamlessly integrated with Christianity, among African slaves in the archipelagos of Central America and in America. Haiti has long been seen as its spiritual center—where roughly half the country's population practices it, in conjunction with Christianity, and where it is spelled "vodou" as per Haitian Creole; henceforth the spelling in the remainder of this chapter.

Haiti officially became a French colony in 1697, coffee production becoming its main economic activity. Slaves were transported from Africa en masse across the ocean to labor-hungry plantations—their numbers reaching 450,000 by the second half of the eighteenth century. Newly arriving slaves were required to convert to Christianity almost immediately. Most Christians of the time saw vodou as a satanic cult, and many of its priests (houngans) and priestesses (mambos) were subsequently killed. Despite such oppression, slaves maintained their traditional religious practices in secret, disguising their "loa," or spirits, as Roman Catholic saints. Indeed, Vodou became an important tool in preserving the slaves' sense of identity and community.

In 1791 a revolution broke out in Haiti against French rule, under the direction of Vodou houngan Dutty Boukman (died c. 1791). Haiti won independence in 1804, becoming the world's first black-led republic. Half a century later, in 1849, President Faustin-Élie Soulouque (1782–1867) crowned himself emperor under the name Faustin I, and raised Vodou to the level of a recognized religion.

Central to Vodou religious practice is the role of objects—from flags called *drapo* to drums, bells, and rattles, from packets of medicinal herbs to dolls—that worshippers invoke to show respect for a loa or else as mediums to contact a loa. A person believed to be possessed is seen as a "horse" being ridden by a loa, and animal sacrifices sometimes also play a role.

In order to curse an enemy or cast a harmful spell, a person can create a doll (the well-known "voodoo doll") that contains a bit of material from the chosen victim, such as a strand of hair or a piece of clothing. This is taken to a sorcerer (bokor), who—if he favorably receives an animal sacrifice also presented to him or her—undertakes the ritual. During the ritual, pins or thorns are pushed into the doll. At those points on the doll that have been punctured, the targeted individual is believed to experience sharp pain. Penetrating the doll's heart or head is thought to kill the victim. Sometimes a piece of string is tied around the doll's neck so that, when tightened, the targeted individual will have difficulty breathing and might even suffocate. The ritual's efficiency is believed to increase greatly if a masterfully punctured doll is placed in front of the victim's door accompanied by a black cross.

But voodoo dolls are not just for Haitians anymore. They have long captured the public imagination, and now, thatnks to the Internet, are widely available to assist all who hold a grudge.

ZOMBIE ATTACK

This brings us to zombie creation. When a bokor undertakes to punish someone, he might use not only dolls but, for good measure, follow this up with zombification. Zombies—which, as we know, are a variety of the undead—correspond to the transitional beings that so imbued the world of myths which prevailed in medieval Europe.

This is how it happens in the popular imagination: The bokor exhumes the targeted corpse from its grave, revitalizing it in several steps that involve injecting it with an elixir that animates it into a zombie. In the third stage, the bokor turns the zombie into a soulless spirit-creature, a servant to do his bidding. The body is not preserved, however, and is thus prone to natural decay, emanating a terrible stench.

In the service of their master, zombies attack their victims unwittingly, and can inflict serious wounds. Occasionally—and so like golems—zombies break free and act independently of their master's bidding, going on uncontrolled binges of destruction and murder (and inspiring an ever-growing thirst for zombie-populated entertainment, from the *Night of the Living Dead* film franchise, to *The Walking Dead* on US cable TV). Survivors of zombie attacks take an unusually long time to heal, and may suffer blood poisoning unless properly treated. Zombies who have reached an advanced state of decomposition will either perish or else continue their undead existence as skeletons.

And this is how it might happen in fact, more or less:

The Bokor creates a "zombie" from a living person through the use of a toxic fluid often derived in part from the puffer fish—a potion that makes him or her who ingests it appear to be dead, and thus the body is often buried. After later retrieving the supposed corpse, the bokor forces it to serve him through tasks that may include physical labor or other, more nefarious ends. The person is sometimes given drugs that conjure a delirious frame of mind while still being able to move about; he or she may end up perishing or suffering brain damage all the same.

Nothwithstanding substantial evidence to support this more rational explanation, many believers do believe that zombies are conjured from the bona fide dead—from those persons whose souls are no longer within their bodies.

In Haiti, zombification, when and where it is practiced, is still regarded by many as the most severe form of punishment, worse even than death. It is the ultimate sanction. A vampire's bite does seem almost benign by comparison.

In 1931 the Hungarian actor Bela Lugosi was immortalized in his now-classic film role as Count Dracula—and yet a little known fact is that a year later he starred in *White Zombie* (See also chapter 29, "Hollywood's Hungarian Dracula."), the film that first popularized the word "zombie." It is a better-known fact that White Zombie was one of the 1990's biggest bands, and that zombies have since migrated from Haiti and gone "mainstream" in Western popular culture.

Chapter 22

Vampires Around the House

Beyond mere gossip and superstition, is there evidence that would suggest that vampires exist, or at least did at one time? Brace yourself for something unusual. The stories that are about to be told here originate mostly in the legends and popular beliefs in Eastern Europe. They record unusual events perceived as supernatural, and were attributed to the influence of demonic beings. The majority of these legends were born in small villages, and then spread through the region by word of mouth. Often they cannot be tied to any real event, having grown out from the soil of religious mysticism, or from the overactive fantasy of a bored villager. The accounts below were adapted by your humble guide from my archival research in Transylvania coupled with material in the works of the noted twentieth-century Hungarian folklorists Enikő Csőgör and Tekla Dömötör.

POSSIBLY TRUE TALE ONE:
A FAMILY AFFAIR

No matter what measures they took for protection, there was a family that was regularly afflicted by all kinds of illnesses and ailments, as the story goes. Continually succumbing to disease, six of their children died in a row. When there was only a little boy left, a traveling medium passed by the village. They consulted him as to what was plaguing them. After much contemplation, the medium took them to the cemetery and after scouting the area he brought them to a grave. A relative of theirs was buried there. While this person was alive, they had been engaged in a long-standing quarrel over a piece of land. The medium advised them to open up the grave

 and examine the corpse. First they were reluctant to do so, not wanting to commit sacrilege by disturbing the peace of the dead, but the medium insisted thy do so. As the grave was opened, they saw to their great surprise that

the dead person's body was perfectly intact, though it should have decomposed long before. The medium pulled out a picket from the cemetery's fencing, sharpened the end, and plunged the stake into the body. As the stake ran through the heart, the dead person let out a piercing scream, and opened his eyes as blood squirted out onto those standing around. He convulsed, and then rose up again. The medium then cut the monster's neck, and let all the remaining blood drain from the body. After the corpse took on the chill of death they said a prayer and put him back into the grave. In a couple of days all remaining members of the family healed from their ailments, which never came back again, and their only remaining child grew up healthy.

POSSIBLY TRUE TALE TWO:
LOCATION, LOCATION

Another source tells of a cemetery-side neighborhood that was terrorized by a vampire. The villagers hung crosses from their windows and ate garlic liberally, yet this did not protect them after darkness fell.

One man was courageous enough to hide by the cemetery's gate and stand watch to discover from which grave the vampire arose. He waited there until the event occurred, late at night. The sight made him stiff with fear, since he saw the devil himself moving among the graves. He suffered no harm, though, because the vampire didn't notice him. The next morning the entire village gathered together to open up the grave he had spotted. It was an old grave, and only a few could still remember that it was the old miller who was buried there. When the coffin was opened, they found an old man's perfectly intact corpse. They consulted the priest about what to do. On his advice they cut out the heart from his chest, which bled abundantly, then lit a fire and incinerated the organ. They mixed the ashes with some water, and each of those present took a sip from the gruesome cocktail. After that the remains of the body were cremated in the fire. Finally they entered the church, engaged in lengthy prayer, then feasted for the next three days. Ritually and physically destroyed, the vampire never returned again.

POSSIBLY TRUE TALE THREE:
AN EYEWITNESS ACCOUNT

It was a terribly chilly winter, and we had burned up all our firewood in the first cold month. One freezing day we took the road by the higher end of the village and went into the woods to cut some branches. The snow was so deep that we couldn't go by carriage, so we travelled on foot, carrying big sacks on our shoulders. I was with my brother, who is shorter than I, but strong. Once we were deep in the woods we heard a terrible shrieking sound, like a dog whining. We got a little scared, figuring it might not be a dog but, rather, a demon wandering around.

Needing the wood, we spent the afternoon cutting branches, then filled our sacks, and turned back towards home. However, before we could reach the edge of the forest, from one of the thickets a huge, gray-spotted wolf sprang out toward us, baring his shining fangs. He jumped right on my brother, knocked him off his feet, and set out to bite his neck. I froze with terror for a moment, but then I pulled myself together and hurried to help my brother, trying to pull the wolf off by its fur. But as soon as I grabbed its fur, the wolf took the shape of a human, turned its yellow eyes toward me, and tried to bite me with its blood-stained jaws. I leapt back, and to my great luck, a sharp-ended stick fell right into my hands, which I stabbed right into its ugly face. I must have wounded it severely, since its blood gushed in spurts. I stabbed it again and again with the sharp-ended stick until it transformed back into a wolf and escaped into the forest. My poor brother had been wounded very badly on his back, and was barely alive as I dragged both of us home through the deep snow, leaving all that good firewood behind.

The next day we returned to the spot. There were bloodstains around the area of the attack. We followed the trail of blood, which led us all the way to the cemetery, to a very old crypt. It was the crypt of a distinguished old family, long died out without leaving progeny. Of course we didn't dare to enter that crypt. We elected instead to consult the priest, who returned with us and performed a ritual cleansing of the spot—all in vain, because two days later the same strange wolf attacked one of our close neighbors. The priest returned to that crypt, had it opened, and had the covers of the three coffins inside removed. To everybody's great surprise, the bodies of the three dead persons were found perfectly intact, as if in deep sleep. The priest ordered the head of each body to be cut off, and then a bulb of garlic placed between the neck and head. We performed this grisly task in silence. This time, the priest's solution was effective, since the wolf never came back.

POSSIBLY TRUE TALE FOUR:
A TWISTED TALE

A house was being built in our neighborhood in the village we lived in. Four workmen were up on the roof doing the carpentry work, while the rest were covering the planks for the walls with mud, which would dry in the sun. They had been working for a long time when one of the carpenters slipped on a beam and fell from the roof. He hit the ground on his back and gave a shout, having fallen on a big stone. His spine was broken. We all rushed around him, but there was nothing to do by watch the life seep out of his eyes. There was loud crying and lamenting, and work stopped at once. We carried the corpse over to the next house, laid him out in the barn, and covered his body out of respect. We sent one of the children to tell his family.

An argument arose over whether or not we should have put him on a carriage to take him home right away. As we were arguing out there in the yard, all at once we saw the dead man come out of the barn, hunched over by his broken spine. There was loud shrieking and commotion. Luckily we had a very learned man with us, who told us right away that the man had transformed into the living dead. He must have been right, because there was no sign of life in his face, and only the white of his eye was showing. Such fearsome monsters had been seen before, and were the cause of great fear among the villagers. Some of the witnesses speculated that a demon must have seized him with its powers, resuscitating him in the form of a devil. But then the learned man told us that we shouldn't let him leave, for he might turn into a vampire. He told us what to do. We gathered out courage and approached the living dead, held him down and cut across the tendons of his legs so he could not walk away. He bled profusely.

Soon thereafter, the family arrived, and he was taken away in a carriage. After a night's vigil he had a decent burial, and was not seen again.

POSSIBLY TRUE TALE FIVE:
DOCTOR, HEAL THYSELF

One day a mystic passed through the village, selling potions. These could be used to heal various ailments, because he was deeply familiar with the healing effects of herbs. Many villagers came out to consult him and purchase his wares. He understood magic practices, both good and bad. He knew the power of curses, and could have made anyone miserable with just a few words. He was talented at all sorts of bewitching and, of course, exorcism.

In a nearby village it turned out that a shepherd had been possessed by the devil. He was very sick, had turned yellowish pale, his hands and legs shook, and he was losing weight rapidly. He went to see a local healer who told him that he was possessed by a devil, which had to be chased out of his body or else he would die. So, through his powers, the man expelled the devil, but must have made some mistake, because the devil did not fully depart, but moved into the wife of the shepherd instead. The woman also became very sick. The healer performed another exorcism, but in such an unfortunate way that this time the devil moved into their young daughter. All further efforts of the healer were in vain, for he couldn't expel the devil from the young girl. Her condition worsened, to the point where the parents began to plan for her burial. Then someone advised the shepherd to take her to the travelling mystic, for he surely knew of some infusions that would heal her.

They went to see the sage, who examined the girl. The girl's mother begged him to give her daughter hope for life. The mystic said the only way to heal her was to perform an exorcism. He began to rub the little girl's body with strong-smelling herbs, then sprinkled water on her forehead as he told the shepherd and his wife to pray as intensely as they could. After he finished with the herb-rub he recited some magic incantations and curses against the devil. Soon after, the little girl started to convulse, until the devil jumped out from her mouth. But instead of going away it turned into wasp and stung the mystic, causing his face to swell up. After the shepherd's family left, the mystic himself got terribly sick. He could not help himself with his own potions, however. He soon became emaciated and died. His body was laid out for two days, but the body disappeared just as he was to be buried. Everyone knew right away that he had turned into a vampire.

THE FEW, THE PROUD

Vampires are created when a spirit is unable to enter the world beyond or, after entering, gets sent back by evil forces. Not just any dead person can become a vampire, only those who had been possessed by Satan during their lifetime. Sometimes these people are said to wear Cain's mark from their birth. Cain's mark might either be a very large, red birthmark, or being born with excessive hair. Other warning signs are being born with eleven fingers or some other mutation, maybe a tail. Newborns cursed by their midwives might also later turn into vampires.

Those who later become vampires have no aversion to blood, and gaze longingly at the wounds of others. They also avoid church and are scared of prayers, crosses, or anything holy. After they are dead, their heads should be separated from their bodies in such a way that the vampire won't be able to refit it on its own. If the vampire does rejoin his head to his body, he will be able to hunt for people's blood once again. Vampires don't only attack people when they are in human form, but they can also take the shape of other creatures: wolves, bats, horses, mice, roosters, and even certain household tools have been accused of vampirism. Vampires are hard to reveal as such, but sprinkling wood ash from time to time on the ground of a cemetery might reveal their footsteps. It is also effective to have a naked virgin ride on horseback all around a cemetery: the horse will jump over any grave except for that of the vampire.

Part IV
Dracula Meets
Popular Culture

JUST A BITE

Chapter 23

Frankenstein

Now that we know all about humunculoi, golems, and zombies, let's pull back a sheet and take a look at one of their gory hybreds, a half man, half monster that, alongside Dracula, is one of the world of horror's all star creations. We are talking about Frankenstein, a creature that has captivated the literary and popular imagination for generations.

The story of Doctor Frankenstein, and the creation of his monster, is exciting enough, but the real-life story of Mary Shelley, author of the novel *Frankenstein*, is almost as exciting. Shelley's maiden name was Mary Wollstonecraft Godwin, and she was born in London in 1797. Her father, William Godwin, of petit bourgeois origins, came to be known as the scandalous writer of the utopian and anarchist work entitled *An Enquiry Concerning Political Justice*. The book, inspired by the events of the French Revolution, supports the creation of a society without social classes, and earned for its author a reputation as the leader of the so-called English Jacobins. In Godwin's utopian socialist views, institutions of the state are unnecessary, and only represent the moral values and habits of bourgeois society. Among other things, he rejected the institution of marriage. His life companion, Mary Wollstonecraft, was seen as one of the first English feminists.

At the birth of her daughter Mary Wollstonecraft died of puerperal (childbed) fever, thus Mary Shelley would never meet her suffragette mother. Soon after, Godwin married a widow, and from that marriage Mary Shelley gained a half-sister named Claire. The two girls grew up in a liberal, free-thinking environment. Mary got the chance to familiarize herself early on with the writings of the Enlightenment era, but she also read a good number of the popular thrillers of the time.

PERCY BYSSHE SHELLEY

The views of William Godwin enjoyed some popularity at the beginning of the nineteenth century. One of his disciples was Percy Bysshe Shelley (1792–1822), a scion of an old aristocratic family who had turned his back on upper-class institutions early on and set out to write verse in which he supported the poor and even urged them to revolt. Due to one of his pamphlets, which was written in an atheistic spirit, and attacked the church and religion, he was disallowed from entrance to all colleges of England—a scandal that put him in the center of public attention. His anarchic views and numerous scandals caused his family to turn their backs on him, but the current periodicals were more than willing to publish his poems. In 1811 the then nineteen-year-old Shelley married the daughter of a bar owner, sixteen-year-old Harriet Westbrook, a few months after he met her. Another major scandal broke out, and the family disinherited the young poet and cut all contact with him. Not wanting to relate this news in person either him or his wife, they published their decision in a newspaper.

The marriage was initially happy, and the still young Harriet Westbrook gave birth to two daughters. At the same time Shelley's popularity was growing, and he forged friendships with many of the outstanding figures of English Romantic literature. In 1914 Shelley met William Goldwin, who also frequented literary circles, and felt an immediate spiritual kinship with him. But the reason he began to frequent Goldwin's household so often was not so much the similarity in their views, but rather his budding love for his daughter Mary. After only a couple months of courtship he ran away with her to Switzerland. From there, he sent a letter to his wife, telling her that he was going to divorce her to marry someone else. Unable to cope with the heartbreak, Harriet Westbrook committed suicide. Shelley was informed of his wife's death only later, by which time Mary had given birth to another daughter. They returned to England to retrieve Shelley's two previous daughters. A court case ensued and it was decided that Shelley's first two daughters would have a better family life with their bar-owner grandfather than with the scandalous couple. Following the verdict Shelley kidnapped the two children, housing them in the same room with Mary's daughter. The consequences were disastrous: disease took the lives of all three. Yet again, Shelley and Mary, afflicted by much suffering, left England to settle down in Switzerland.

In 1816 Mary and Percy Shelley befriended fellow exile and English poet Lord George Noel Gordon Byron (1788–1824), who was by then enjoying international fame for his art. Living close to each other, they got together frequently, and on rainy days they often passed time by telling stories. On one of these occasions Byron suggested that they organize a literary contest among themselves. The idea was that each of them should write a parody of the then-popular thrillers. This fateful evening was re-imagined in Ken Russell's film *Gothic*.

Lord Byron and Percy Shelley never did

complete their works for this little contest of theirs, but Mary did. In a matter of only a few days she created the outline of a well-rounded story by the title *Frankenstein, or the Modern Prometheus*. Although Mary had originally intended to write a parody, the result was so good that her husband suggested that she publish the novel. The work of the nineteen-year-old woman became an international success, and one of the most enduring examples of the literary horror genre.

A MONSTER SUCCESS

The main character is the young and talented Victor Frankenstein, who studies mathematics and chemistry at the University of Ingolstadt, in Bavaria. The ambitious young scientist contrives to create a flesh-and-blood human being in his laboratory. For his project he uses body parts from various corpses, and by accident he chooses the brain of a criminal.

As all horror fans know, his creature ends up looking monstrous, being of towering height, with veins that can be seen through his translucent skin, and of course with a repulsive face. Doctor Frankenstein brings him to life using electric current, but being taken aback by his horrid ugliness, quickly flees in terror. Frankenstein's monster comes to consciousness alone in a messy and stinking room. He puts on Doctor Frankenstein's gown and sets out to wander aimlessly in the forests of Bavaria. He lives on berries and roots, having no idea why the people he accidentally crosses paths with are so terrified of him—until he sees his own image reflected in a pool of water.

The monster, tortured by loneliness, is unable to grasp how he came into this world, and what is to become of him.

On a particularly cold winter's night he takes shelter in the barn of a house on the edge of a small, remote village. From there he secretly observes the everyday life of the three people who live in the house: a blind old man, a melancholic youth, and a beautiful girl. Being endowed with considerable natural intelligence, little by little he comes to understand human speech, and pilfering some books, even learns how to read. Having developed a fervent love for the three people, he becomes—through reading and listening—more and more educated and self-conscious.

Being unable to suffer his loneliness any longer, he decides to reveal himself. In the absence of the younger people he approaches the blind old man, who is unable to see his ugliness. But the young ones return, and in their repulsion, they chase the monster away. In his disappointment, the monster that was until now basically good, and hungry for love, becomes resentful, bitter, and violent.

The monster decides to seek out his creator, Doctor Frankenstein, whose journal he came across by accident in the pocket of his gown. From that journal he discovers the circumstances of his creation. He sets out, intent on holding the good doctor responsible for his suffering.

The monster wanders across Switzerland in the direction of Geneva, the city where Doctor Frankenstein lives. Along the way he has two terrible encounters. In the first, he saves a little girl from a flooded river, but when the father notices the girl in a monster's arms, he shoots, wounding him gravely. He manages to escape, and suffers badly from his wound, cursing his creator and mankind as a whole. Nevertheless, he tries to come to the aid of a little boy lost in the mountains, and who just happens to be the brother of Doctor Frankenstein. The child becomes terrified of him, calling him an ugly devil, and attempts to flee. The monster, scared of the child's shrieking, tries to silence the child, but accidentally strangles him. Doctor Frankenstein is the only one to witness how his brother died, but holds his tongue. The boy's nanny is accused of the crime, and she is executed.

Frankenstein's monster finally meets his creator on a mountain ridge, where they are both filled with reproach.

The monster asks Doctor Frankenstein to create a female companion for him. With her, he hopes to leave the human world and go live in a remote, uninhabited land. Hearing of the humiliating experiences the monster went through, Doctor Frankenstein abandons his desire to take revenge for the death of his little brother.

To fulfill the monster's request, Dr. Frankenstein retires to a remote corner of the Orkney Islands, and prepares to create the female monster. The new creature is only half finished when the scientist realizes that from the marriage of this couple a new race would emerge—and become a menace to mankind. Horrified, he abandons his project.

In his disappointment, the monster extracts

a terrible revenge. He plots to methodically kill the friends and relatives of Doctor Frankenstein, to take the life of his love, and drive his creator mad. In the tragic ending, both monster and scientist degenerate into madness. The monster, who starts thinking of

Doctor Frankenstein as his father, though he never even received a name from him, ends up retreating into the mystic and frozen world of the Arctic Sea, followed by Doctor Frankenstein, who again seeks revenge. Before he can catch his creature, the ship is frozen in the ice and he dies of exhaustion. The monster shows up at the coffin of his creator, and promises the captain of the ice-locked ship (the narrator of the whole story) to end his pitiful existence by committing suicide.

It is not hard to detect numerous elements of the golem myth in Mary Shelley's novel. At the same time, her thriller raises some important questions, while also offering pathos and excitement to the reader. One of these questions is whether science could be seen as all powerful, and whether scientists have the right to intervene in life as godlike creators. But the most important question raised seems to be whether human creations might turn out to destroy human beings, and whether good intentions might tragically reverse into evil ones. As they say, "The road to hell is paved with good intentions."

It was Mary Shelley's life experience that made her sensitive to these profound themes. But her personal tragedies were not over yet. Not long after the publication and enormous success of her work, she lost her husband, who drowned in the Adriatic Sea during a sailing trip. Percy Shelley, twenty-nine, was buried by his friend Lord Byron. Byron himself died two years later in Greece, where he had traveled on impulse to join the Greek freedom fighters in their rebellion against the Turkish occupation.

FRANKENSTEIN'S PROGENY

Left without a family, Mary Shelley administered her husband's literary estate until her own death in 1851, all the while creating other works of literature. None of these became as successful as the Frankenstein story, though her 1826 novel *The Last Man*, with its apocalyptic depiction of the extinction of mankind, does carry considerable artistic and philosophical value.

Frankenstein appeared in a talking movie for the first time in 1931, when American director James Whale brought it to the silver screen. He gave the role of the monster to the British actor Boris Karloff, who hair-raisingly played the physically and psychologically pathetic, love-hungry monster. After the great success of the original movie, a sequel followed. In 1935 *Bride of Frankenstein* appeared, followed by *Son of Frankenstein* in 1938. In the latter film the son of the deceased Frankenstein, named Wolf, travels to his father's castle, where he discovers that the monster is not dead, after all, only sound asleep in one of the remote chambers. He revives the monster at the insistent pleading of a hunchbacked caretaker. This initiates a series of mysterious deaths, and the young Frankenstein's life also becomes endangered, though he ultimately manages to rid mankind of this menacing monster once and for all.

This ending did not allow for any continuation to the story, but due to the relentless public interest a great number of the story's details were subsequently brought to the screen or retold in novels. One particularly memorable homage was the cult movie and musical *Rocky Horror Picture Show* from 1974, which drew on, along with the golem myth and Mary Shelley's Frankenstein story, various elements of musicals, horror, and soft-porn films. In this story a young couple, Brad and Janet, seeks help when their car gets a flat tire. They wander into a nearby ramshackle building, where they are greeted by a horde of curious creatures led by a devilish transvestite. The strange inhabitants are celebrating an anniversary, and as the main attraction of the program they bring to life by electroshock an artificial man, who is named Rocky Horror. Terrible as the monster might seem, what comes afterward is not a series of cruelties as with the original Frankenstein (except perhaps the reviews delivered by priggish film critics), but rather some strange mix of a rock-and-roll party and an orgy.

As with the example of the Frankenstein story, the vampire of the medieval popular imagination had firmly made its way, by the beginning of the nineteenth century, into high culture. In fact literary references of this nature first appeared in the second half of the eighteenth century, when the first known poems about vampires appeared.

As mentioned earlier, in 1816 a small society of writers gathered in a villa on the shore of the Lake Geneva to hold a horror story contest. On this occasion Lord Byron started writing his own vampire story, though he left it uncompleted. The unfinished manuscript ended up in the hands of Doctor John William Polidori, Byron's physician. He finished the story, and published it in 1819 under the title *The Vampyre*. The main character of the original text, whom he baptized Lord Ruthven, appears in his version mimicking Byron's physical traits and manners. Even some elements of Byron's biography were also attributed to the protagonist. In this satirical portrait Polidori ingeniously transformed Byron into a bloodsucking vampire! And so the first vampire-man of high literature was created as a poet-like figure, sensitive to art and altogether superior to ordinary humans (and, it is safe to say, he is a precursor to Stephenie Meyer's touchy-feely vampire Edward Cullen, of Twilight fame). *The Vampyre* was published to great success at around the same time as Mary Shelley's *Frankenstein*. Soon it was brought to stage in many theaters across Europe. The avid public interest led to an opera version not long after. Nevertheless, the vampire figure did not entirely penetrate popular culture until Bram Stoker's *Dracula* was published in 1897.

Bram Stoker retained many elements of the literary version of the vampire myth, but managed to make it accessible and palatable for a mass audience. From the publication of his book on, the development of the vampire myth took different paths in high literature and in popular culture, carrying different meanings, while using a common set of symbols.

Chapter 24

The Doctors of Fear

Nineteenth-century romantic art and literature was particularly preoccupied with depicting the struggle between good and evil. Simultaneously, the industrial revolution was taking place, and the technical innovations and scientific achievements it offered transformed people's everyday lives. The new developments in the natural sciences and in medicine met with the admiration of the public, but at the same time those who professed traditional religious values felt a growing unease. Doubts about the power of science were based on the supposition that any intervention in the order of nature might liberate not only positive, but also evil forces. Scientists and doctors might acquire powers that they could use for both good and malicious purposes.

Romantic literature reflected all this by depicting a scientist or doctor who has unusual, supernatural powers, and using these unleashes demonic and satanic forces on his environment. The prototype of this figure already existed in medieval literature in the form of witchdoctors, gold-making alchemists, fortune-tellers, and sorcerers. These figures of the Middle Ages undoubtedly involved themselves with evil forces, but in the case of their modern counterparts that intent is not quite so obvious. The main question addressed in these works is: "We humans are good. So why don't we do good?"The main question was, in other words, how good intentions can produce evil results. Attempts to answer it have varied over the centuries. Rousseau said that humans are good by nature but spoiled by civilization. Existentialists were to claim that the human condition is in itself absurd and meaningless—that man is a corrupt, purposeless being. Indeed, the horrific events of twentieth-century history made some thinkers see humans as the most destructive of all beings.

THE STRANGE CASE OF
DR. JEKYLL AND MR. HYDE

The Scottish novelist Robert Louis Stevenson (1850–1894), in his 1886 novel *The Strange Case of Dr. Jekyll and Mr. Hyde*, presents in the person of Dr. Jekyll, a well-respected, rich, and successful doctor from London—a deeply religious person who spends much of his money on charity, but who is at the same time aware there is a darkness lurking in his personality. Moreover, he discovers that there

are actually two persons living inside him. He tries to reconcile this split by making the evil side "disappear." He invents a magic potion, and by drinking it manages to move the bad side of his character into the monstrous Mr. Hyde. This enables him to impress everyone by his goodness and unselfish generosity, while by turns taking the appearance of Mr. Hyde to exercise his brutality and pursue hedonistic pleasures. At first he can keep this situation under control, but later Mr. Hyde takes the upper hand, and Dr. Jekyll turns into this evil creature more and more frequently, despite taking the antidote. Transforming into the embodiment of evil, and losing his original human character, the doctor ends up escaping only through suicide.

Legend has it that Stevenson penned his novel in a matter of three days under the amphetamine effect of cocaine. This is thus also an example, similar to the story itself, of how a destructive temptation might lead to a strong and ultimately invincible addiction.

Stevenson's work is in fact the tale of a split consciousness. While those stories that recount the creation of a *homunculus* (such as Frankenstein) place the evil monster outside of the human being, Stevenson's book finds the infernal being *inside* the human soul. That is to say, the heart of any person equally carries the possibility of both good and evil. God and the Devil may coexist every human being. Although these beings have no external powers, they are held in constant struggle inside the human soul, trying to get the upper hand and direct a person's behavior. In Stevenson's view it is not an external evil that possesses a person, but rather it is the person who discovers the devil that dwells within his soul, and who liberates this power—a process that can unfold in a number of different ways. This devil might burst to the surface as a demon, vampire, zombie, or merely an evil alter ego, while simultaneously striving for beauty and human life.

CALLING DR. CALIGARI

In the German silent film titled *The Cabinet of Dr. Caligari* (1920), written by Carl Mayer and Hans Janowitz and directed by Robert Wiene, the main character uses his evil supernatural forces to keep a medium named Cesare—who has an ability to foresee the future, and has been living in a world of dreams since his birth—under his full control. The doctor and his companion, Cesare, settle down in a sleepy German town, where they make their living as showmen. After their arrival, the small town witnesses a series of murders. A local young man called Francis starts investigating the death of his friend, and soon he suspects Dr. Caligari and Cesare of the murder. When he goes to see them, he finds Dr. Caligari standing vigil, while Cesare is lying in the coffin that serves as his bed, in a deathlike trance. All this is the appearance, though, since Cesare is a split personality, and the other side of his soul is just trying to get the beloved lady of Francis under his control. After Francis realizes what happened to his love, he pursues Dr. Caligari and the medium after they flee. The investigation leads him to a psychiatric institution, where he discovers that the real criminal is the director of the clinic, who uses a patient as a medium to relive the monstrous deeds of another Dr. Caligari who lived two hundred years ago.

By bringing this story to the silver screen, director Robert Wiene became the founder of expressionist cinematography. The characters of his movie are either mentally insane, or puppets with no will, acting under hypnosis—all of them split personalities, as it were, whose demonic self took the upper hand, with fatal results. The illusions and tricks of the human mind, that make everything relative, only add to the nightmarish atmosphere.

A novel by French author Norbert Jacques

titled *Doctor Mabuse the Gambler* deals with the world of the human beings who stray from the reality of everyday life and are thus tempted by evil. Doctor Mabuse is an exceptional criminal who is able to multiply his personality and appear in varied disguises, all the while using hypnotic persuasion to steal people's money. More than monetary wealth, he desires to gain the fullest possible control over his victims. With his demonic forces Doctor Mabuse turns people into puppets deprived of their own personalities and unable to act according to their own will. An attorney, who is the only person able to resist to his evil tricks, manages to reveal his wrongdoing. But Doctor Mabuse ends up falling victim to himself, as his personality disintegrates to the point that he goes mad.

This story was brought to the screen in 1922 by Fritz Lang (1890–1976), a master of the early German cinematography. In an interview given in the early 1930s Lang hinted that the figure of Doctor Mabuse might be construed as a representation of Adolf Hitler. Lang shot a sequel in 1933 under the title *The Testament of Doctor Mabuse*. In this continuation, the insane Doctor Mabuse lives in a grim cell of a psychiatric institution. Gradually he gains control over the institution's director, transforming him into a puppet serving his will. Several terrible, satanic crimes then occur in the clinic's neighborhood. Doctor Mabuse dies, but the clinic director believes himself to be his reincarnation, and the series of crimes continues. Finally a detective arrives, and discovers the insane director in the cell where Doctor Mabuse once lived. Because of its political overtones the movie was banned in Germany, so the first screening took place in Vienna. Not much later, Fritz Lang had to move to the United States, escaping from Nazism.

Chapter 25
Fantômas

The character Fantômas is a mysterious apparition of an undetectable nature. A spirit who is capable of assuming any form, he might appear in turns as a handsome young man, a wealthy gentleman, or a white-haired elderly person. From the world of spirits, he can easily access the material world, only to retreat just as easily whenever he decides to. This ability allows him to do things us common mortals are unable to, such as passing through walls. Fantômas is the most intelligent of all criminals, and in his time, committed a number of unsolved murders. Surrounded by a special aura, he is able to cast such a powerful charm on his victims that they hasten to forgive him for all his crimes.

The character was created by two French journalists, namely Marcel Allain (1885–1969) and Pierre Souvestre (1874–1914). The story became the basis for a stream of popular novels in the early 1900s. The enduring interest of the public was such that a total of thirty-two sequels were written. The world of cinema was also quick to exploit the character; the first Fantômas movie was shot by French director Louis Feuillade (1873–1925) in 1913. In this movie Fantômas appears as an unscrupulous criminal, who is not only the

embodiment of the evil, but also a curiously attractive being who can see into the most hidden domains of the human soul. Constantly changing his form, he appears in a variety of masks, all the while remaining an illusive spirit, leaving the talented and smart Inspector Juve no chance to apprehend the slippery Fantômas.

The first Fantômas film was an incredible success, for it allowed moviegoers to project their own fears and anxieties onto the character, and at the same time to revel in an erotic, mystical, and thrillingly violent story—all of these aspects breaking the taboos of the day. Yet despite all his brutality Fantômas remained a sympathetic figure, who opposed to all the values and customs of the petit bourgeois.

THE FANTÔMAS INDUSTRY

Encouraged by the great success of the first movie, Feuillade shot four sequels of the Fantômas story in the years 1913–14. These met such success that their creator engaged himself further with the representation of mystical and hair-raising topics, and in 1915 started a new series under the title "Vampires." Through the 1920s, the adventures of Fantômas continued both in novels and on the screen. The tense political and social atmosphere of the 1930s and the horrors of World War II then diminished the public's appetite for made-up monsters, and Fantômas was discontinued, but only temporarily. He made a comeback in the 1960s, when André Hunebelle shot his movie *Fantômas* starring two legendary French actors, Jean Marais in the role of the spirit and Louis de Funes as Inspector Juve. Mysticism and terror are less present in this newer movie, which featured Louis de Funes as an absentminded and awkward detective, while Fantômas was re-interpreted as a gangster who is not only charmingly seductive but whose exploits are also humorous and quite easy to forgive. Hence, material that was originally almost mystical and terrifying was treated this time more lightly, resulting in a parody of the costumed adventure movies and detective movies of the times. This was especially true for the subsequent continuations—which appeared through the 1960s, after the initial great success of the Marais/Funes casting.

The figure of Fantômas became so well known in popular culture that many believe today that the name, rather than referring to a specific figure, is rather a sort of general term that could be applied to any elusive and cruel criminal who seems impossible to catch—a phantom of supreme cunning. Fantômas has been transformed into a symbol of human unscrupulousness and unfulfilled evil wishes. Despite all his cruelty, his person also offers a sort of pardon and reconciliation—namely, by suggesting that *none* of us is innocent.

Chapter 26
Vampires and Classic Cinema

The history of motion pictures goes back to 1895, when the Lumière brothers—Auguste Marie Louis Nicolas (1862–1964) and Louis Jean (1864–1948)—patented the cinematograph, an invention that allowed the projection of film. The silent movies shot in those early days were brief, and it was enough to document mundane contemporary events to thrill audiences. Fictional films came into fashion soon thereafter, though the first example also came in that first year, 1895, with Louis Jean Lumière's comedy *L'Arroseur arrosé* (also known as *The Waterer Watered* and *The Sprinkler Sprinkled*).

One of the most important early filmmakers, who started his career along with the birth of cinema itself, was Georges Méliès (1861–1938). Originally a stage director and actor, he shot his first film in 1896. The next year he opened a studio in Montreuil, close to Paris, and by 1913 he had created some 500 films. His success was due mostly to the visual tricks he innovated, which represented the first "special effects." Always open to new material to exploit, in 1896 he conceived of and directed the first vampire film, *The Haunted Castle*. This was not the one that made his name famous, though. Recognition came through his film *A Voyage to the Moon*, which some count as the first science fiction movie.

Méliès's vampire film made an impact at the time, drawing the attention of several movie directors to the topic. Bram Stoker's *Dracula* and Méliès's work in fact appeared in the same year, starting the genre of horror on its long march of popular success.

Film production during World War I waned, though newsreel documentaries grew in popularity. In the years following the war moviemaking made a comeback, and it was not long before Dracula was drawn upon for source material. The first film version, however, appeared not in the West, but in a place near Dracula's Eastern European homeland that still suffered the effects of the war—namely, Russia. In the aftermath of the Russian Revolution, 1918–1921, before the communists had firmly secured power, artistic life still enjoyed relative freedom. This was beneficial not only to Russian literature and art, but also to the first wave of Russian cinema.

The folkloric themes of Dracula likely struck a special chord with Russian filmmakers, as vampire myths were prevalent in the popular beliefs of eastern Slavic cultures. Very little information exists regarding the Dracula movie shot in 1920, as all its copies were soon lost, and it was never screened in the rest of Europe.

A year later, in 1921, the Hungarian movie director Károly Lajthay made a new Dracula movie, which followed Bram Stoker's novel only in broad strokes, adding a number of original twists and modifications. This movie made no real impact with the public, and though it was screened in Austria and in Germany, it was soon forgotten. (See Chapter 28, "The Dracula Film that Time Forgot.") The 1922 Dracula adaptation by the German director Friedrich Murnau, under the title of *Nosferatu*, however, was an instant international success, thanks to its creative visual innovations and atmosphere. (See the next chapter.)

The late 1920s and early 1930s marked a turning point in the history of cinematography, as the black-and-white, silent movies were gradually replaced by talkies. Color technology followed not long after. A new era dawned for horror films as well, when two great actors, Boris Karloff and Béla Lugosi, in 1931, starred in two talkies, respectively playing Frankenstein and Dracula. The two creations set a high standard for the representation of evil in film, initiating a new wave of horror movies.

By the 1960s the well-exploited Dracula canon was rich for parody. The most successful one of these was created by Roman Polanski. A master of psychological crime stories and horror movies, Polanski first became well known in 1961 for his horror film entitled Knife in the Water. Similar creations followed, such as *Repulsion* (1964), *Cul-de-Sac* (1966), and *Frantic* (1988). His unmistakable morbid humor came across most fully in T*he Fearless Vampire Killers or: Pardon Me, But Your Teeth Are in My Neck.* Shot in 1967, it showed off not only his directorial prowess but also his acting talent, while his wife, Sharon Tate—who two years later would meet her real-life end in horrific fashion at the hands of followers of Charles Manson—starred in the lead female role. The film tells the story of a vampire-hunting professor who travels to Transylvania together with his assistant, in search of actual vampires. After many adventures they finally arrive at Dracula's castle, where vampires are gathering in preparation for their traditional annual ball. The vampires are scary and ridiculous at the same time, as are the vampire hunters, ably satirizing the canon of vampire films that preceded it, as well as those to come. (See also Chapter 30, "Vampire Blockbusters.")

From the 1970s on vampire films took many different directions, attesting to the sustained public interest in them. In addition to parodies, some versions mixed in elements of black magic, Satanism, sexuality, and even pornography. TV adaptations appeared, as well as some romantic versions of the classic tale of Dracula. One outstanding movie on the topic released at the end of the decade by Werner Herzog was a remake of *Nosferatu*, starring Klaus Kinski.

Then, through the 1980s, public interest in classic horror subsided somewhat, giving way to horror movies that featured spectacular visual effects or depicted serial killers who stalked teenage victims. Interest in vampiric exploits on screen returned thanks to a 1992 movie by Francis Ford Coppola: *Bram Stoker's Dracula*. The fantastic visual effects of this ambitious movie revived the cult of the vampire myth, and directors to this day look to it for inspiration.

Chapter 27

Nosferatu

One of the most influential representatives of early German cinematography was Friedrich Wilhelm Murnau (1888–1931). He began his career as a theater specialist, briefly working as an assistant to the world-famous stage director Max Reinhardt. He got into filmmaking after World War I. His interest as a movie director was centered, from the very beginning, on the fantastic, successfully utilizing the tools of silent movies in his depiction of evil. This talent was on display in one of his earliest works, the Satanas, shot in 1919. Two years later, in his movie *The Haunted Castle*, he returned to his unique style of shooting long close-ups of facial expressions to underline the narration. Facial expressions were used to follow the flow of emotions and to escalate tension, allowing the audience to empathize with characters good and evil, a technique he would later apply to his famous vampire.

In his movies the borderline between real and

unreal is murky, reality becoming interwoven with dreams. In 1922 Murnau shot *Nosferatu: A Symphony of Horror*—the first important vampire movie in the history of film.

This movie follows the narrative of Bram Stoker's novel, though screenwriter Henrik Galeen added some of his own ideas. The vampire's name was changed from Dracula to Nosferatu because Murnau did not hold the movie rights to the novel. However, this did not keep Bram Stoker's widow from taking Murnau to court for using the story without permission. At the end of the trial the court decided that all copies of the movie should be destroyed. Indeed they were burned (so like a witch at the stake) except for one reel, which survived, much to the good fortune of the history of cinematography.

In the story a real estate agent from Bremen sends his young and recently married bookkeeper, Thomas Hutter, to Transylvania, to the castle of the Orlok counts, hoping he can settle some business. On arriving he witnesses a series of hair-rising sequences—seeing first horses, then wolves and eerie-looking birds emerge from the milky white fog. On his journey Hutter takes a rest in an inn, where he is warned to beware of Count Orlok. The bad omens intensify when a book about vampires accidentally falls into his hands in the inn, and he learns some unsettling things about their nature. His coachman is unwilling to continue the journey, terrified as he is of vampires.

Just when it seems his mission is at an end, the count's black carriage shows up to shuttle Hutter to the castle. In the mysterious castle, Count Orlok receives his guest courteously. Since dawn is approaching, they retire to bed. The next morning Hutter cannot find his host, so he searches around the castle for him. Crossing eerily empty halls, he finally discovers the count lying in a sarcophagus with a deathlike expression and open eyes staring out into emptiness. The shaken Hutter realizes in that moment that Count Orlok is in fact Nosferatu, the vampire. Tormented by fear and doubts, Hutter is already thinking of escaping when darkness falls again and his host awakens. Nosferatu attacks Hutter and—in classic vampire style—bites his neck to suck his blood. Hutter manages to escape, thanks to his wife Ellen who, by some telepathic sensitivity, awakens from her dream back in Germany, and yells her husband's name at the very moment he is bitten. Taking advantage of this fleeting moment in which Nosferatu is stunned by the power of love, Hutter escapes the castle and flees back to Germany.

Nosferatu pursues Hutter, traveling by day in a coffin. Wherever he passes, rats swarm, spreading the plague and causing people to drop dead. At last Nosferatu voyages on a ship to Bremen. The rats overrun the ship as well, causing the crew to die. The ghost ship continues its way on its own, carrying the corpse of the vampire as its ghastly cargo. In the meantime, back in Bremen, Hutter's wife discovers the book about vampires in her husband's luggage. Recognizing the danger about to menace her city, she fearlessly sacrifices herself by attracting Nosferatu and spending the night with him, all to keep the deadly disease from spreading through Bremen. Nosferatu is so charmed by the innocent woman that he forgets about the arrival of dawn. Ellen directs the morning sun onto him, reducing him to a heap of dust. Death awaits Ellen as well for having spent the night with a vampire, though she manages to save her city through her bodily sacrifice. Murnau leaves the end of the story open, the woman's final fate untold.

In 1978 Werner Herzog remade *Nosferatu*. In his version, Nosferatu is not only a personification of horror, but also a vulnerable being who suffers infinitely from loneliness. Modern filmmaking technology allowed Herzog to create a truly ghastly atmosphere. The opening images of the movie were shot in Mexican catacombs, where various mummified human corpses are found leaning against the walls with their mouths open as if they had died in a state of terror. Equally powerful scenes follow this strong opening, with Klaus Kinski's outstanding performance in the role of Nosferatu. Unlike Murnau, Herzog did not leave the end of the story open. In his version the woman dies of her encounter with Nosferatu, and the vampire regenerates. The movie thus suggests that evil lives forever. This ending allows us to continue the myth and its different variations in our imaginations. The "Symphony of Horror" hence still resounds and is eternal.

Chapter 28
The Dracula Film
that Time Forgot

Popular belief holds that it was first Friedrich Wilhelm who brought Dracula's story to the silver screen in *Nosferatu, the Vampire*. This is not quite true, though, since the Hungarian silent movie *Drakula halála* (*The Death of Dracula*) appeared one year earlier, in 1921. According to some sources the director, Károly Lajthay, wrote the script in 1920 based on Bram Stoker's novel but complemented it with some original ideas by film critic and journalist Lajos Panczel. Moreover, the script found a collaborator in Mihály Kertész (1886–1962)—better known as Michael Curtiz—who would become famous and win the Oscar some twenty years later for directing *Casablanca*.

The story contrived by the writers takes place in three locations: a village in the Alps; a psychiatric institution in Vienna; and, finally, the castle of Dracula. The main narrative thread regards a poor seamstress named Mary Land, whose father was confined to a psychiatric institution after being unable to accept the death of his wife. Mary visits her father regularly, and among the patients she meets is Dracula, a supposed music teacher, who naturally sparks her interest when he claims to be immortal. It is in Mary's nature to take everything, even the words of the insane, seriously. Indeed, two other patients, disguised as doctors, convince her that she is seriously ill, and she nearly undergoes surgery at their hands as a result.

Mary, exhausted from her misadventures, spends the night at the hospital. Dracula takes advantage of the situation, and absconds with her to his castle, where he dresses her in a bridal gown. Dracula invites evil spirits to the wedding, a ceremony during which he plans to bite the girl. Mary, however, awakens, and repels Dracula with the help of the cross hanging from her neck, after which she escapes from the castle. Wandering through the snow-covered forests, she all but freezes to death. Fortunately, she is rescued by locals, who call a doctor to assist, and is thus saved.

But Dracula appears again, making a second attempt to spirit the girl away. This time it is the doctor who repels the attack. The story ends happily, with the help of both the cross and medical science.

Dracula returns to the psychiatric institution in the hope of finding another victim, but a patient shoots him dead in a fit of madness—and, thank goodness, he does in fact die.

Lajthay's movie was produced at Budapest's legendary Corvin Film Studio, with Paul Askenas in the role of Dracula and Lene Myl playing Mary. It is open for debate as to whether Vienna or Berlin was used for the street scenes in the film, but by the standards of the film technology of the era, *The Death of Dracula* was a grandiose endeavor.

For reasons that remain unclear to the present day, the movie had a negligible international career despite an auspicious premier in 1921 in Vienna. It was not screened abroad again for a long time, and in Hungary it debuted only in April 1923. A small company bought the rights to the screening, making but scant efforts to promote the movie through newspaper ads. Hungary's political situation at the time might have also contributed to the public's lack of interest—namely, the fact that in the years following World War I, the cultural products of those smaller nations that had been on the losing side in the war were not particularly sought after.

HUNGARIAN CINEMA'S EARLY RISE & FALL
—AND DRACULA'S DEATH

Hungarian audiences saw their first motion picture in 1896, when the representatives of the Lumière brothers held a screening in Budapest's Hotel Royal. This was also the year their country saw the production of its first newsreels, primarily focusing on the celebration of the nation's upcoming millennium. From that time on, motion pictures were screened in Hungary intermittently in cafés, in dance halls, and under circus tents. Budapest's first real cinema opened its doors in 1906. The first Hungarian film was shot in 1901. A movie studio, Hunnia, opened in 1911. And a year later the nation's first full-fledged motion picture drama was made under the direction of Mihály Kertész, titled *Ma és holnap* (*Today and Tomorrow*).

Aside from Budapest, the only other city then in Hungary where movies were shot regularly was in Kolozsvár, known as Cluj-Napoca in Romania—which was to annex that city from Hungary with the rest of Transylvania after World War I. This is where the career of the great film producer and director Sándor Korda (1893–1956)—better known as Sir Alexander Korda—began, to continue later in Great Britain.

Hungarian cinematography had discovered its own talents and found its modes of expression by the end of World War I. This flourishing industry was sadly paralyzed by the country's military defeat. No wonder that by the end of the 1920s Hungarian film had lost its greatest talents to emigration.

The uncertainty of the times might be the reason that Lajthay created *The Death of Dracula* with Austrian and German cooperation and held the premier in Vienna. Few copies were made of the movie—all of which seem to have been lost during World War II. Only the accounts of the contemporary newspapers, and a novel adaptation written by Lajos Pánczel, can give us some idea of what the film might have been like.

Chapter 29

Hollywood's Hungarian Dracula

Since all modern vampire stories have their roots in the popular imagination of Eastern Europe, it seems natural that the first movie versions sprang from the same territory. From the dawn of film, moviemakers have seen possibilities in the cinematic interpretation of the vampire myth, even in the era of the silent movie. After talkies appeared, film studios in Hollywood took the lead in the adaptation of the stories, enriching time-honored legends with a host of new elements.

Hollywood's most renowned Dracula was without a doubt the legendary Hungarian actor Béla Lugosi (1882–1956). Lugosi's acting talent was recognized early on, and from the age of twenty he had already played a number of major roles in Budapest's National Theater. He was immediately sought after in the silent film business for his expressive face and ability to mimic emotions. Wanting to separate his theatrical career from his cinematographic activity, he appeared in the movies under the pseudonym Arisztid Olt.

Soon, though, history interrupted the promising rise of his career. During World War I—a vibrant period for Hungarian cinematography—Lugosi starred in a great number of movies, most of which were unfortunately lost in the turmoil of the era. Toward the end of the war, the idea of nationalizing Hungarian film studios arose, and met with sympathy in cinematographic circles, as this was seen as a possible solution for their financial troubles. The defeat Hungary suffered in the war, however, led to social unrest. The nation's new political leadership had more pressing troubles to resolve than improving the state of Hungarian cinematography.

The communist revolutionary government that took power briefly in Hungary in 1919 carried out a long series of nationalizations, and cultural institutions were no exception. "Cultural directorates" were established for the supervision of these now state-owneed institutions, and among their members were the greatest artists of the time: composer Béla Bartók, director Mihály Kertész, and actor Béla Lugosi. Artistic activity of the time could not escape the influence of the dominant political ideology, and so the movies shot during the short reign of

the regime—some thirty of them—were all painfully didactic. After the fall of the communist regime, and the coming to power of the rightwing forces under the leadership of Miklós Horthy (who was to lead Hungary as regent into World War II), reprisals against the members of the cultural directorates followed. This in turn led to a wave of emigration among artists. The nation's once fast-developing cinematography stagnated, and only revived again toward the end of the 1920s, under government control.

BÉLA LUGOSI, THE VAMPIRE LOVER'S VAMPIRE

Béla Lugosi, fearing reprisal for the political role he had played, emigrated to Vienna, from where he then moved on to Berlin. After a couple of years he made the bold decision to move to the United States and try his luck in Hollywood. After starring in a handful of silent films, his breakthrough role came when he was cast in the role of Dracula. His interpretation had such a deep effect on the American public that the Dracula persona became synonymous with this actor. Another effect of the film's popularity was that Transylvania became immediately associated far and wide with Dracula and vampires. In Bram Stoker's novel, most of the action takes place in England, referring to Transylvania only as to Dracula's country of origin: a mysterious and distant land. By contrast, this spectacular movie sets presented the region of the Carpathians as a desolate, cold, and grim environment, a place that thus became the homeland of vampires in the public consciousness.

American film director Tod Browning shot his talking version of *Dracula* in 1931, starring Béla Lugosi in the main role. The movie was an interpretation of Bram Stoker's novel, albeit with many additions and changes. Lugosi's distinguished appearance and unmistakable accent made him very convincing in the role of Dracula, and the incredible effect brought him much deserved praise and success. Curiously, Lugosi had only a tenuous command of English, and needed to memorize the script phonetically.

In the movie Lugosi played a suffering creature who, unable to find peace in death, has no choice but to rise from the grave every night and feed on human blood. Lugosi interpreted Dracula as a sensitive soul endowed with magical powers, who is constantly surrounded by a mystical aura of immortality. Finally the vampire hunter, after a long series of horrific scenes—in which Lugosi presented the creature's innate evil with outstanding credibility—manages to prevail over the monster.

Unfortunately, the public identified Lugosi so heavily with the role of Dracula that moviegoers would not accept him in any role that strayed too far from the horror genre. One exception was the comedy entitled *Ninotchka*, shot in 1939 by the director Ernst Lubitsch, who purposely chose to cast actors against type. The main character was played by Greta Garbo, known to the public as a melancholic femme fatale, who for the first time in her career laughed on screen. Similarly, Lugosi was assigned a comedic role. Ninotchka made a sensation but was not wholly successful. In the same year Lugosi returned to horror, starring in the final part of the *Frankenstein* trilogy, in the role of Igor, the hunchback servant.

From the 1940s the life and career of Béla Lugosi took some tragic turns, and in his final years he became addicted to alcohol and morphine. When he died in 1956, at the age of seventy-three, as per his will he was buried in the black gown with red satin trimming that he had once worn in the role of the vampire Dracula.

Chapter 30

Vampire Blockbusters

Those Dracula films with Béla Lugosi in the title role reigned for a long time as horror classics of the silver screen. By the 1950s and 1960s, however, a dearth of vampire movies set in. But from the late sixties on, several exceptional directors facilitated a new flowering of the genre that has continued to this day in numerous directions and with ever larger audiences flocking to see the latest blockbusting bites. Vampires have, indeed, branched out well beyond traditional horror into other film genres— including fantasy, satires, action, and, in recent years, films with pronounced romantic-erotic themes and films directed toward young adult audiences (often overlapping subgenres). Dracula in his (or her) many guises has also conquered television, with several hugely successful series.

DRACULA RETURNS WITH A LAUGH

It is Roman Polanski who can be credited as the first major director to herald the return of the vampire film—with his 1967 comedy horror classic *The Fearless Vampire Killers or: Pardon Me, But Your Teeth Are in My Neck*. At first this film, which injected humor into the otherwise traditional story of two vampire hunters who venture into Eastern Europe—Professor Abronsius and his apprentice Alfred—at first registered hardly a splash in America. And yet two years later, after the murder of the female lead, Sharon Tate (Polanski's wife) by followers of Charles Manson, the producers once again introduced the film, which now proved to be a huge success. Its popularity has been so consistent even since then that in 1997 it was adapted into the musical *Dance of the Vampires*. In 1995, Mel Brooks, with his movie *Dracula: Dead and Loving It*, took to an absurd extreme what Polanski had started. Here, Dracula, played by Leslie Nielsen, is the world's most dangerous creature because those who see him die immediately—of laughter. The legendary count heads off on his nightly prowls, and yet he winds up being hunted himself by a professor with state-of-the-art tools; and he can no longer take even himself seriously. The year 1995 saw yet another vampire satire—*Vampire in Brooklyn*, with Eddie Murphy in the lead and directed by Wes Craven.

ACTION, PLEASE

Action films came to the fore in the 1980s, with such an emphasis on spectacle that in fact the sustained pacing of the action itself often suffered in result. Vampire myths proved an ideal match for this genre—one of the most original examples being Robert Rodriguez's *From Dusk Till Dawn* (1996), written by Quinton Tarantino. Quintessential Tarantino, this movie is marked by witty dialogue, bloody and violent action, and exceptional casting. Embracing various genres, it is both a Western and a vampire film, and it is, moreover, spiced with comedy.

The 1998 superhero action film *Blade*, starring Wesley Snipes and based on the Marvel Comics character Blade, was such a success that it went on to see two sequels. Bitten by a vampire during her pregnancy, the protagonist's mother bears a son, Blade, who is a human-vampire hybrid destined to protect people from vampires. With the help of his friends, he has been fighting vampires since birth to take vengeance for his mother's death in childbirth. Frost, a vampire who leads a renegade faction that sets out to rule humans (and, indeed, harvest them) ultimately engages in battle with Blade.

This trilogy—*Blade*, *Blade II*, and *Blade: Trinity*—represented two key innovations to the vampire film genre. Not only did it feature beings in part human, in part vampire, but the human-vampire Blade fights throughout for good against evil—creating a new movie myth, that of the good vampire.

Complementing the classic adventure genre with action scenes, *Dracula 2000*, directed by Patrick Lussier and starring Gerard Butler, preserves all essential elements of traditional vampire myths while at the same time focusing not so much on plot but, rather, on bringing out the bloodiest possibilities from each scene. The year 2003 marked the debut of the vampire/werewolf film trilogy *Underworld*, which contained numerous allusions to Hungarian history—for example, the name of the character Alexander Corvinus, who has three children. One kid, Marcus, is bitten by a vampire, and so he becomes the first vampire. His twin brother also has rotten luck, being bitten by a wolf—and so he becomes the first lycan (i.e., werewolf). The third son gets off without a bite, though one of his descendants, Michael Corvin, a doctor, winds up being the first vampire/lycan hybrid. That's the story in just a bite.

Beyond its heart-racing scenes, the 2004 action horror film *Van Helsing*, starring Hugh Jackman and Kate Beckinsale, sought to capture audiences by linking the story of Dracula to other classic horror tales.

Van Helsing, the celebrated vampire hunter, works for the Vatican's Knights of the Holy Order, a secret organization charged with destroying evil.

At the outset, Van Helsing is in Paris, where he manages to free Dr. Jekyll from the wicked Dr. Hyde. He then returns to the Vatican, where he is given his new mission: to go to Transylvania and help hunt down Dracula. Meanwhile, Doctor Frankenstein happens to be in Transylvania, too—in Count Dracula's castle, of course, where he is busy trying to give life to his creations cobbled together out of corpses. Naturally, Dracula is supporting Frankenstein's experiments not out of goodwill, but so that he might use the creature to his own nefarious ends. When Doctor Frankenstein realizes Dracula's plan, he resists and tries to kill Dracula; but he is fated to be the victim, for Dracula cannot be killed, seeing as how his heart is already dead. Meanwhile the creature escapes, taking refuge in a windmill that the locals set ablaze—which, it seems, will scuttle Dracula's designs. In the meantime who arrives on the scene but Van Helsing, and with this turn of events an epic struggle ensues.

LOVABLE VAMPIRES

The lacing of vampire movies with romantic, erotic

content got underway in a big way in 1994 with the film adaptation of Anne Rice's best-selling novel *Interview with the Vampire*—a movie whose success was thanks in no small part to the casting of sex symbols Tom Cruise, Brad Pitt, and Antonio Banderas. At the outset of the story is an interview given by a two-hundred-year-old "young man" about his life to a journalist. The man recounts how he won immortality, which is however increasingly a burden to him. Beyond the film's stunning visuals, its key point of interest is that director Neil Jordan departed from traditional vampire stories in putting the emphasis on the question of whether immortality is worth it if it means becoming a solitary carnivore. In contrast with most of the vampire fare that had been on the world's menu until then, this novel portrayed vampires as suffering, sensitive, beautiful, erotic beings forced beyond their will into wickedness. Poor things.

Indeed, Anne Rice's book and its film adaptation saw an avalanche of new takes on the age-old mainstream vampire myth. Writers who have followed in her footsteps—other women prominent among them—have given birth to a new romantic hero: the forever young, gentle, beautiful, and erotic vampire who is, deep down, *good*. A vampire capable of battling against other, wicked forces. No few such vampires follow a strict "non-human" diet, too, in that they do not drink human blood, but rather the blood of animals or synthetic blood.

Such tales might even be seen as parodies of the original vampire myth, but this is not the case, for this newfanged [sic] theme became one of the "deadly" serious core ingredients of these works. And from here it took but one more step for the world to arrive at yet another watershed moment—vampire myths for kids or, rather, teenagers.

One of the most successful of these romantic vampire works has proved to be *The Twilight Saga*—the five fantasy films based on Stephenie Meyer's *Twilight* novel series, which recounts the story of a girl named Isabella "Bella" Swan. At the series' outset her mother remarries, and Isabella decides to move in with her father, a police chief in the small, rain-forest-cloaked town of Forks, Washington. In her new school Isabella is received with open arms, with one notable exception: Edward Cullen, a boy who is outright antagonistic toward her, but whom Bella falls in love with almost immediately. Frightening rumors swirl about Edward and his family among those living on the Indian reservation near town. The more Isabella gets to know this boy, the more his secrets are exposed, and the more she falls in love with him. In the end not even Edward can keep his distance from her, and indeed he shares with her his greatest secret—no need for a spoiler here: it's obvious, isn't it?—and lets her get to know his own family, er, coven. . . . But with this, the Isabella's life falls into great danger. The series hit international bestseller lists, but its detracters find Meyer's metrosexual vampire extra creepy in his habitual stalking of Bella, and due to the fact that instead of withering in sunlight, he sparkles.

And, if you think that's cool stuff, consider Seth Grahame-Smith's 2010 book (and the 2012 film) *Abraham Lincoln, Vampire Hunter*, which gives American history a whole new twist with its sensational revelation that, in fact, the fight against the South—and slavery—was a fight against vampires.

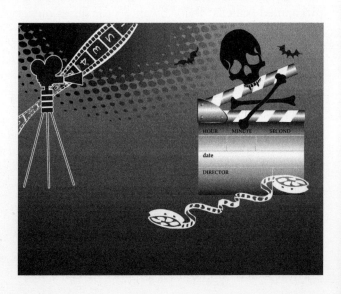

Chapter 31
The Book of Dracula

Doing so might not seem in keeping with chrono-logical order, but what better way of concluding *Just a Bite* than with paying homage to Bram Stoker's *Dracula*? Besides, other vampire fads come and go, but the impact of this staple continues to resonate to this day among vampirologists young and old.

Written by Irish author Bram Stoker and pub-lished in 1897 in England, this novel was instantly a resounding success. The secret of its popularity lay in the fact that the author could fill the relatively simple action of the book with atmospheric, creepy settings and complex characters, foremost Count Dracula himself. The novel brought the vampire myth into the public consciousness, so it's not surprising that the hit book was adapted for other forms of art as well. From Stoker's work numerous plays, movies, cartoons, and even ballets have been derived. Stoker also revisited the material, publishing the sequel titled *Dracula's Guest* in 1913.

The fact that all vampires are measured against Count Dracula illustrates the measure of the book's reach. It is, then, worth investigating what Stoker's sources of inspiration and documentation were. After some analysis it can be stated that what he in fact wove together four separate threads, the first one being the historic character of Vlad the Impalor. This element was not a prominent one, however, as Stoker had very limited knowledge of Vlad III, and practically none of Wallachia, the country Vlad had ruled. Few historical works were available in England that Stoker could have used to learn about fifteenth-century Romanian history. At the same time he was somewhat familiar with Transylvania as a geographic setting and a historic backdrop, having read a book Emily Gerard published about the region in 1888, under the title *Land Beyond the Forest*. Ultimately, this became his main inspiration in choosing the setting of his story.

The other thread, or rather source of inspiration, was a series of presentations in London made by the Hungarian Orientalist scholar, Ármin Vámbéry (1832–1913). A devoted researcher of Eastern cultures, Vámbéry had spent years in Istanbul and was well-versed in the history of the Balkans beyond having a far-reaching knowledge of Turkish history. He had developed such a sterling reputation as an "Asia" expert that both the British and the Turkish governments sought out his advice. At the time Stoker first started considering writing a book based on the story of Dracula, Vámbéry happened to be in London giving a series of presentations on Eastern European folklore. Stoker attended one of them, and what he heard there impressed him so much that he went to visit Vámbéry in his hotel room that very night and engaged him in a long conversation. It is known that they met several more times during Vámbéry's stay in England.

From Vámbéry, Stoker learned much about certain aspects of Eastern European vampire lore. The vampire as a character of cultural history and also as a literary subject was not previously unknown to Stoker, whose literary sensibilities were however shaped in part by Samuel Taylor Coleridge's long poem *Christabel*, whose action is underscored by a sense of mysticism, by a demonic presence that likewise influenced Edgar Allen Poe. Stoker had also read works based on vampire mythology, and was deeply impressed in particular by the popular opera by Silvestro Palma (1754–1834), *I Vampiri*.

The three threads mentioned thus far—the history, Vámbéry's presentations, and other literary works—were animated by a fourth: Stoker's own imagination. It was his creativity that transformed Dracula into not only a Transylvanian nobleman but also an immortal, bloodsucking aristocrat. According to literary scholars, Stoker's mind had been further stimulated by the mystery of the serial murders committed by Jack the Ripper, and also by the friendship he made with literary man and explorer Richard Burton, who had just translated eleven Hindi vampire stories into English.

THE DRACULA BRIEF

As the story of the novel goes, a young law clerk by the name of Jonathan Harker, called upon to settle a business affair, sets out to travel across Europe so he can meet with the mysterious Count Dracula, currently living among the Transylvanian mountains. As he nears the count's castle, the scenery becomes increasingly disquieting, foreshadowing the events to come.

The castle is grim and almost uninhabited, yet Harker's fears are dissipated by the warm welcome his host makes for him. But in the castle he gets to know the count's real nature, through a series of increasingly spine-chilling experiences. There are a growing number of warning signs that the count is not what he seems, such as the incident when Harker and Dracula are both standing in front of a mirror, but only Harker's reflection is visible. Dracula ends up capturing and confining Harker, then departing for London in order to spread the cult of vampirism. Harker manages to free himself and also returns to England, with the goal of preventing the count from carrying out his diabolical plan. Alone he would be powerless, but to his good fortune he crosses paths with Dr. Abraham Van Helsing, a Dutch expert in vampirology and an experienced vampire hunter familiar with the techniques of exterminating these creatures. It is only with his help that Harker finally manages to rid his country of the lurking danger embodied by Count Dracula.

Stoker, in line with the tastes of the Romantic era, also infused the mysterious and disquieting events with an erotic charge. Take for example the scene when three young female acolytes of Dracula surprise Harker in his bed, awakening within the young protagonist a desire for sensual experience. It was this unique mix of mysteriousness, adventure, and blood-curdling description, along with raw sensuality that ensured the novel's success—while inadvertently spreading any number of misconceptions concerning the historic setting of Transylvania among readers. These misconceptions have become so deeply rooted in our era that the historic Dracula's reputation as a "real vampire" from Transylvania has almost solidified into fact.

Chronology

c. 1000

Deeply religious Christian Europe was awaiting the arrival of the Apocalypse and the Last Judgment. Those preparing for the end of the world tried to fortify themselves in body and spirit to the fight against evil. Numerous writings of the time espouse the supernatural powers of certain individuals or otherwise deal with witchcraft and otherworldly creatures such as ghosts and sprites. Ironically to the modern mind, the failure of the Last Judgment to arrive was interpreted as the victory of Satanic forces.

1047

A Russian document uses the word upir—a reference to a cruel, murderous prince—that would later transform into the word vampire.

c. 1100

An increasing number of historical records mention witch hunts and witch trials. In Hungary, the legal code of Kálmán the Book Lover (c. 1074–1116) declares that witches do not exist and therefore should not be persecuted. But was Kálmán himself a witch? Vampire legends begin to spread among the Slavic nations of Eastern Europe and the Balkans.

1190
Vampire legends make their way into Western Europe. A twelfth-century source entitled *De Nagis Curialium*, by Walter Map, retells some of these stories.

1196
In his work *Historia rerum Anglicarum* or *Historia de rebus anglicis* (History of English Affairs), William of Newburgh includes tales in which vampires are conceived of as souls who return from the dead.

c. 1200
The Inquisition initiated by Pope Innocent III (1198–1216) persecutes heretics, alleged witches, and other individuals supposedly empowered with magical forces.

1202–1204
A crusade serving the interests of Venice seizes Constantinople. Stories common among the peoples of the Balkans thus spread among the crusaders, including accounts of vampires.

Mid-thirteenth century
A procedure for investigating accusations of witch-craft is set, and women convicted of the crime of being a witch are burned at the stake.

1326
In Hungary, with the participation of King Charles Robert, the order of Saint George is founded, aiming to follow the example of the martyr Saint George (c. 275/281–303), whom legends hold to have defeated a man-eating dragon.

Mid-fourteenth century
The Romanian principalities of Moldavia and Wallachia take shape and stabilize politically, creating a link between the Balkans and the eastern Slavic territories. Popular beliefs concerning vampires, werewolves, and the living dead gain force especially among the Vlachs (Romanians) of Wallachia.

1408
Hungarian king Sigismund of Luxembourg (1387–1437) creates the *Order of the Dragon* with the intention of defending true faith against pagans and heretics.

c. 1420
A son of Mircea, the Prince of Wallachia

(1387–1418), named Vlad, and raised in the Hungarian royal court, is accepted into the Order of the Dragon and takes up the name Dracul (meaning Dragon). His name is to become a crucial element for the Dracula myth. Vlad Dracul is given an estate in Transylvania by King Sigismund.

1428/29
Presumably in Sighişoara, a son is born to Vlad Dracul, and is named Vlad. Later to become known for his horrible deeds, he is to be nicknamed "Ţepeş" by his contemporaries, meaning "the Impalor." His figure became the foundation of the legend of Dracula.

1435–1447
Vlad Dracul reigns in Wallachia. Opposing the Ottoman Empire, he is imprisoned, and subsequently beheaded by the Turks in 1447.

1456
With assistance from the Hungarian leader, Vlad Ţepeş ascends to the throne of Wallachia. Subsequently he leads several successful campaigns against the Turks.

1462
In the course of a military campaign against the

Turks, Vlad Țepeș falls from power. Seeking refuge in the Hungarian royal court, he is held captive by King Matthias Corvinus, and remains there for thirteen years.

1477
Regaining his freedom, Vlad Țepeș returns to Wallachia in order to regain the throne, but falls victim to a conspiracy.

1486
An envoy of Ivan III tsar of Russia (1462–1505), Fiodor Kuritsin, writes the first account of Vlad III, the historical Dracula, depicting him as a monarch who promotes justice, but is at the same time cruel and autocratic.

First half of the sixteenth century
An increasing number of sources deal with the horrible deeds of Vlad Țepeș. These first appear in Austria, but soon spread to almost all countries of Western Europe.

1560
Birth of Elizabeth Báthory, later known as the "Monster of Csejte," or the "Blood Countess."

1610

Leo Allatius publishes his work entitled *De Graecorum hodie quirundam opinationabus*, which includes the first description of the modern vampire.

1610

Elizabeth Báthory is convicted of having tortured hundreds of servants, killing them, and bathing in their blood. She lives for four more years, confined to a room in Csejte Castle.

1610–1630

Gábor Báthory, Prince of Transylvania, and his sister Anna are accused of having committed incest. After her brother is killed, Anna faces four consecutive witch trials and loses her fortune, but is allowed to live. Sources all across Europe deal with the Báthorys' nefarious reputation.

1657

Francoise Richard publishes a treaty by the title *Relation de ce qui s'est passé a Saint-Erini Isle de l'Archipel*, underlining the connections between witchcraft and vampires.

1672

Large-scale vampire hysteria breaks out on the Istrian peninsula among the region's Italian and

Croatian inhabitants. Buried corpses are unearthed and burned, and several people suspected of being vampires are lynched.

1679

Philip Rohr's De *masticatione mortuorum* is the first work to be published in German language about vampires.

1710

Vampire hysteria sweeps across Eastern Prussia. Numerous cemeteries are dug up, and a mob sets the houses of suspected vampires on fire.

1725

A new and even larger wave of vampire hysteria unfolds in Eastern Prussia, claiming numerous victims.

1725–30

The hysteria that originated in Eastern Prussia spreads to other areas of Eastern Europe, soon reaching Hungary.

1725–1732

In the southern territories ruled by the Austrians, inhabited mainly by Serbians, several people are sentenced to death on charges of vampirism.

1734
Through translations of German (especially Eastern Prussian) sources, the word "vampire" first appears in the English language.

1735
Spanish physician Gaspar Casal is the first to describe the disease pellagra, which has "vampire-like" symptoms.

1744
Giuseppe Davazanti, an Italian cardinal, publishes a comprehensive work on vampires under the title *Dissertazione sopre I Vampiri.*

1746
Augustine Calmet publishes the vast study titled Dissertations sur les Apparition des Démons et des Esprits, et sur Revenants, et Vampires de Hongrie, de Boheme, de Moravie et de Silésie, dealing with Hungarian, Moravian, and Silesian vampires.

1748
German author Heinrich August Ossendelfer writes the first modern poem on the vampire myth, *Der Vampir.*

1750

A new outbreak of vampire hysteria in Eastern Prussia reawakens Europe's attention to the topic. The wave of the hysteria reaches Eastern Europe, just as happened before, culminating in Wallachia.

1798

Samuel Taylor Coleridge writes *Christabel*, the first English poem seen by many as based on the "vampire" myth.

1800

The Milan opera stages Silvestro de Palma's *I Vampiri*.

1810

In northern England rumor has it that a sheep has been killed vampire-style—its veins cut open and its blood sucked out. In reaction John Stagg publishes his poem *The Vampyre*. He goes on to write more poems on the topic.

1820

The Vampire, the first such theatrical play, is staged in London, based on an English translation of French author Charles Nodier's *Le Vampire*.

1829
Nodier's story is translated into German, and Heinrich Marschner writes an opera based on Nodier's Le Vampire, which is presented in Leipzig, Germany.

1854
Interest in vampires reaches America, with a widely publicized alleged vampire attack victimizing the Ray family in the small town of Jewell, Connecticut.

1872
In Italy a man called Vincenzo Verzeni is convicted for having killed two people and drinking their blood.

1874
According to an account from the town of Ceven, Ireland, several sheep are found with their throats cut open and their blood sucked out.

1888
Emily Gerard publishes a description of Transylvania under the title *Land Beyond the Forest*. Bram Stoker will later use this book as inspiration when setting his novel *Dracula* in Transylvania.

1897

Bram Stoker's *Dracula* is published. Its sweeping success will define all further development of the vampire myth.

1912

In Great Britain the first movie with vampire characters is shot under the title *The Secrets of House No. 5*. Since no copies remain, it is only known through descriptions from contemporary publications.

1913

Bram Stoker's new novel, *Dracula's Guest*, is published.

1920

Bram Stoker's novel *Dracula* is brought to the screen for the first time in Soviet Russia, but amid the turbulent, post-Revolution times all copies of the movie are lost.

1924

Fritz Harmann, known both as the "Butcher of Hannover" and the "Vampire of Hannover," is convicted in December of killing, vampire-style, more than twenty boys and young men. He is beheaded the following spring.

1927
The stage version of Stoker's novel debuts in London. In the same year it is also presented at the Fulton Theater of New York City.

1942
A. E. Van Vogt's *Asylum* appears. The first book to feature an extraterrestrial vampire, it sees the vampire theme filter for the first time into science fiction.

1954
Publication of Richard Matheson's science fiction novel *I Am Legend*, set in a future Los Angeles swarming with undead bloodsucking cannibals.

1958
The publication, in the United States, of the book *Famous Monsters in Filmland* revives interest in the horror genre.

1962
Donald A. Reed creates, in the United States, the *Count Dracula Society*.

1964
Two TV series featuring vampires (*The Munsters* and *The Addams Family*) are launched in the United States.

1965

Jeanne Youngston creates the *Count Dracula Fan Club* in the United States.

1970

Sean Manchester founds the Vampire Research Society in the United Kingdom.

1972

The movie *Vampire Kung-Fu* is shot in Hong Kong, the first work to associate the vampire myth with martial arts.

1972

Radu Florescu and Raymond T. McNelly publish their work *In Search of Dracula*, which addresses the historic figure of Vlad Țepeș.

1972

Stephan Kaplan creates the *Vampire Research Center*.

1973

Nancy Garden's book *Vampires* introduces vampires to young adult literature.

1975

Fred Saberhagen launches the first periodical aimed at vampire fans, *The World of Dark Shadows*.

1976
Anne Rice publishes *Interview with the Vampire*, the first in her bestselling series the Vampire Chronicles, which has sold more than 80 million copies worldwide.

1977
The Vampire Studies Society is founded in Chicago by Martin V. Riccardo.

1979
With its song *Bela Lugosi's Dead*, the British band Bauhaus introduces the vampire theme into rock music, becoming an inspiration for the Goth movement.

1980
The Bram Stoker Society is created in Dublin, Ireland.

1980
The "Vampire of Sacramento," Richard Chase, convicted of killing six people in cannabistic and Draculalike fashion only a year earlier, commits suicide in his cell.

1989
Following the death of Romanian dictator Nicolae
Ceauşescu, Transylvania becomes accessible to the
Dracula fans from abroad. Romania is subsequently
subject to considerable renewed interest in the
Dracula myth.

1991
A role-playing game called *Vampire: The Masquerade*
takes the world by storm.

1992
Andrei Tchikatilov from Rostov, Russia, is convicted
for killing fifty-five people "vampire style."

1997
Buffy the Vampire Slayer debuts on network TV in
the United States.

2000
A variety of vampire role-playing games appear on
the Internet.

2000
The International Dracula Festival takes place in
Sighişoara, Romania.

2002
Vampire hysteria breaks out in Malawi, Africa. The population of the southern territories migrates north, escaping from a supposed vampire invasion.

2005
The first of the *Twilight* series of vampire romance novels, by Stephenie Meyer, is published.

2010
Publication of Seth Grahame-Smith's book *Abraham Lincoln, Vampire Hunter*.

2012
Mexican "Vampire Woman" Maria Jose, whose extreme body modifications include implanted fangs, body piercings, and titanium horns, becomes an international media darling and a champion in the fight against domestic violence.

Glossary

This glossary is broad, but neither comprehensive nor encompassing all approaches to vampirology. With all due respect to phenomena such as role-playing games that have drawn many into the fold of fantastical vampiric universes in recent decades, it is geared more toward that which has been firmly part of the Western cultural cannon for centuries, along with a smattering of must-know facts from more popular culture that have shaped millions of minds. Hence, look online or elsewhere for terms like "awakening," "blood doll," "coven," "elder," "The Hunger," and "kindred." Included are mythological and religious terms whose resonance has indirectly shaped our conceptions of vampires and their undead cousins—indeed, these have been widely adapted by today's role-players and "vampire lifestyle" adherents—as well as people, places, and concepts from history and folklore, some of which are described in more detail in the main text.

Aerope
In Greek mythology, the lover of Aeres (the god of war). Although she died in labor, her dead body continued to nurse her newborn.

Akh
An ancient Egyptian concept of the dead that ranged from the intellect as a living entity to a ghost of sorts that could be either benevolent or malevolent.

Ba
A key component of the human soul in Egyptian mythology, one's Ba was thought to survive after the body died and was often portrayed as a human-headed bird.

Báthory, Elizabeth (1560–1614)
One of the most famous figures in vampire lore— notorious as a serial killer, organizer of lesbian orgies, host of cannibalistic feasts, and someone who bathed in the blood of young maids. Despite a dearth of evidence, her reputation as the "Blood Countess" grew until she became a symbol of human cruelty.

Beelzebub
A Semitic deity that in Christian and biblical references was to occur as a synonym for Satan— and that in demonology is a prince of Hell.

Black Death

Spread by a flea-borne bacteria, bubonic plague killed some 25 million people in fourteenth-century Europe and millions more in later centuries. Some believed that vampires buried alongside innocents in mass graves were responsible, gorging themselves on flesh—and blood—before climbing out to wander again among the living.

Bloodletting

A core practice of medieval medicine rooted in the belief that bodily fluids carried sickness, and that these fluids sometimes had to be expelled. It stretches back to Antiquity and may have helped shape our conceptions of blood as regards vampires.

Blood libels

Pervasive myths in Europe over the centuries used to justify the persecution of Jews. A common allegation: Jews would kill Christians, often children, in sacrificial rituals and mix their blood into the matzos they prepared for Passover.

Blood oath of the Hungarians

In the ninth century the seven Magyar (Hungarian) tribes, in quest of a new land, made a blood oath generally regarded as Hungary's first, unwritten constitution. Each chieftain cut his arm and let his blood flow into a horn, which they then drank from. Such practices have been common among other peoples through history.

Bran Castle

Was this gothic castle near Braşov, Romania, a refuge for the same Vlad III who acquired the Wallachian throne and was banished to Transylvania for a time—Count Dracula? The evidence is slight, but popular belief has long had it that it was the scene of unspeakable acts of terror at his hands.

The Cabinet of Dr. Caligari

In this 1920 German silent horror film (dir. Robert Wiene), the protagonist uses his evil powers to keep a medium named Cesare under his control. The small town they settle in sees a series of murders.

Cacus

A firebreathing giant and the son of Vulcan in ancient Roman mythology, he lived on human flesh, nailing his victims' heads to the doors of his cave. He was killed by Hercules.

Cerberus

Most typically known as the three-headed dog in Greek and Roman mythology that guards the gates of the underworld.

Charon

In Greek mythology, the ferryman of Hades who transports the souls of the newly departed to the world of the dead.

Chimera

This fire-breathing female monster from Greek mythology—depicted as a lion, with a goat's head rising up out of its back and a tail capped off by a snake's head—is defined more broadly as any mythical creature comprising parts from various animals.

Csejte Castle

Today the ruins of a castle near Čachtice (Hungarian: Csejte), a village in western Slovakia (formerly Hungary) that in the late sixteenth and early seventeenth centuries was the home of "Blood Countess" Elizabeth Báthory—and, after she was accused of horrible crimes, became her virtual prison.

Demon

Rooted in an ancient Greek term Latinized as *daemon* or *daimon*—which referred to benevolent nature spirits—this concept later took on negative associations, with the Judeo-Christian "demon" referring only to evil spirits.

Dracula
Bram Stoker's 1897 gothic horror novel that popularized the character of the vampire Count Dracula. Stoker had limited knowledge of the historical Vlad III, and practically none of Wallachia, the region Vlad ruled in the fifteenth century. For this and other reasons, Transylvania became his setting. In 1913 he published the sequel *Dracula's Guest*. See also **Vlad III**.

Drakula halála (*Dracula's Death*)
Count Dracula's first appearance on the silver screen? Released in 1921, a year before *Nosferatu: The Symphony of Horrors*, this lost Hungarian classic (dir. Károly Lajthay) was a liberal adaptation of Bram Stoker's novel. See also *Nosferatu*.

Dumuzid or **Dumuzi ("the Shepherd")**
A king in Sumerian mythology who was said to have ruled for 36,000 years. The husband of Inanna, the Sumerian goddess of sexual love, fertility, and warfare, he was taken to the netherworld as Inanna's substitute after she was allowed to return from there.

Echetus
The king of Epirus in Greek mythology, described in the *Odyssey* as the "destroyer of all mortals" and as

having blinded his own daughter and locked her up in a tower.

Edimmu
In Sumerian mythology, the vengeful spirits of those who were improperly buried. Believed capable of sucking the life out of people—especially those who were young and asleep—they were also thought to cause disease and criminal behavior in the living.

Elysian Fields
As seen by many ancient Greeks, the world beyond for heroes and others favored by the gods. Later imagined more broadly as the realm where the blessed find bliss in death.

Empusa
A beautiful demigoddess of Greek mythology who seduced young men as they slept, then drank their blood and ate their flesh.

Erra
The warlike Akkadian god of pestilence

Fantômas
Created by two French journalists at the turn of the twentieth century, this fictional character was

a mysterious apparition of an undetectable nature that could assume any form. It became the basis for a series of popular novels in which it operated as a savvy criminal whose aura cast a powerful charm upon its victims.

The Fearless Vampire Killers or: Pardon Me, But Your Teeth Are in My Neck

Directed by Roman Polanski, this 1967 film—which brought (morbid) humor to the vampire genre— tells the story of a vampire-hunting professor who travels to Transylvania with his assistant in search of vampires.

Frankenstein

The protagonist of Mary Shelley's 1818 novel is young Doctor Frankenstein, who, using corpses, creates a flesh-and-blood human that comes to life as a monster. A series of events follow in which a creature that was until then basically good, and hungry for love, becomes vengeful and violent.

Gilles de Rais (1404–1440)

A French contemporary of Vlad the Impaler whose reputation likewise had an effect on the formation of vampire legends. As with some other "real life" vampires (see **Elizabeth Báthory**), the question arises: Did he really commit the terrible crimes he was accused of?

Golem

Medieval Jewish folklore used this biblical word to refer to a moving being made of inanimate matter. Kabbalistic tradition tells stories of legendary rabbis who knew how to produce robotlike servants from clay mixed with human blood, using a sacred word of command. See also **Homunculus, Rabbi Judah Loew ben Bezalel,** and **Zombie**.

Harpies

In Greek mythology, these winged spirits (sisters of Iris) stole food from King Phineus. Initially described as beautiful, by Roman and Byzantine times their ugliness was renowned, as it was in the Middle Ages. In Dante's *Inferno* they appear as ugly women with wings, and popular culture has maintained their reputation as weird, violent beings.

Hecate

An ancient, often three-headed, three-bodied goddess of magic, witchcraft, the night, the moon, ghosts, and necromancy. With roots in Anatolia, she made her mark in Greece and Rome and is today commonly viewed as the goddess of witches. Shrines to Hecate were placed at doorways, city gates, and crossroads in the belief that doing so would keep the restless dead and other spirits at bay. She sometimes has a dog or dogs at her side.

Heka
The deification of magic in Egyptian mythology.

Hematophagy
The practice among many species—including various insects and leeches—of feeding on blood. Human societies have also partaken of this, whether by mixing cow's blood with milk, in the form of black pudding, or drinking the blood of slain enemies. The Christian Eucharist evokes hematophagy, the mentally imbalanced have been known to practice it in horrific ways, and of course many of us are apt to lick our wounds.

Homunculus
Latin for "little man," the term was used by the Swiss-German physician, botanist, alchemist, and astrologer Paracelsus (1493–1541) to refer to an artificial creature created through alchemy. It has been used broadly in various disciplines to refer to the representation of a human being, and its manifestation in Jewish folklore is the tiny, fully

developed person at the core of Golem legends. See also **Golem** and **Rabbi Judah Loew den Bezalel.**

Hydra
In Greek mythology, a multiheaded serpentlike aquatic creature with toxic breath.

Ichor
An ancient Greek term for the blood of the gods, which was believed to ensure immortality. A drop was enough to give birth to new gods.

Impalement
One of the least pleasant execution methods of medieval times, excelled in by the historical figure most associated with Count Dracula, Wallachian ruler Vlad III (posthumously known as Vlad Ţepeş; i.e., Vlad the Impaler). A pointed stake would be inserted into the victim's anus, then pushed up the colon and along the spinal column. The stake was then made to come out between the neck and the shoulder blades, after which it was stuck into the ground.

Incubus
A male demon that, in various mythological traditions, descends on and has sexual intercourse

with women as they sleep—repeated exposure to which can cause ill health or death. The female version is the succubus.

King Kálmán I
This Hungarian king (c. 1074–1116)—commonly known in English as Coloman I and nicknamed "Kálmán the Book Lover" because of his literacy and education—is famous for having outlawed the persecution of witches. But was he a witch himself?

Lamia
In Greek mythology, a beautiful queen who became a child-eating demon. Seen in modern times as half-human, half-snake. Mothers across Europe once kept their little ones in line by invoking Lamia.

Leviathan
A biblical sea monster that, in demonology, is a prince of Hell and its gatekeeper.

Lidérc
A malevolent spirit unique to Hungarian folklore. Its three overlapping forms include, most prominently, the "miracle chicken" (*csodacsirke*), hatched from a black hen's first egg warmed under a human arm. Then there is the earthly devil (*földi ördög*); and the "devil's lover" (*ördögszerető*), manifesting itself as a

ghostly nighttime light—that is, a will o' the wisp, a cousin of what in English is traditionally known as a jack-o'-lantern.

Lilith
Possibly related to a class of female demons in Mesopotamian texts, Lilith was known in Jewish folklore from the 8th–10th centuries onward as the biblical Adam's first wife, who eventually mated with the archangel Samael. The associated legend has made its mark on modern Western literature and popular culture.

Lugosi, Béla
Hollywood's iconic vampire, Lugosi (1882–1956) played the title role in Tod Browning's 1931 film *Dracula*. His distinguished look and (Hungarian) accent brought him praise, but also served to typecast him as a villain.

Matthias Corvinus
Under the constant menace of the Ottoman Turks, Wallachian ruler Vlad III (the Impaler) was obliged to accept help from this legendary Hungarian king (1443–1490), and indeed was his virtual prisoner for years.

Mephistopheles
The demon to whom Faust sells his soul in the classic

German legend Faust, Mephistopheles was adapted by Goethe in his tragic play *Faust* and has appeared as a devilish figure elsewhere in literature.

Minotaur
A creature from Greek mythology with a bull's head on a man's body—one that fed on human flesh—the Minotaur was to become a compelling presence also in twentieth-century fantasy fiction.

Moroi
In Romanian folklore, a vampire or ghost embodying the spirit of those who died after being excommunicated.

Morpheus
The god of dreams in Greek mythology, Morpheus is a winged daemon that assumes human form and appears in dreams.

Mot
A West Semitic god of death, this favorite son of the god El was the god of all forces opposed to life and fertility—in contrast with his arch enemy, the god Baal.

Namtar
A minor deity in Mesopotamian mythology, Namtar

was the god of death and disease and a messenger of the underworld.

Nosferatu: A Symphony of Horrors
Released in 1922 (dir. Friedrich Wilhelm Murnau), this was the first major vampire movie in the history of film. Remade by Werner Herzog in 1978, it was an unauthorized adaptation of Bram Stoker's novel *Dracula*.

Order of the Dragon
The epithet "Dracul" was first embraced by Vlad II (c. 1393–1447)—prince of Wallachia and Vlad the Impaler's father—after he joined this order founded in 1408 by Sigismund, King of Hungary (1368–1437). The order's initiates were charged with defending Christianity, especially against the Ottoman Turks.

Pellagra
A disfiguring disease that reached epidemic proportions at the turn of the eighteenth and the nineteenth centuries. Caused by a nutritional deficiency, it causes lesions on those areas of skin most exposed to sunlight—hence the possible association in the public imagination with those dreaded creatures of the night, vampires. It also led to disorientation, restlessness, insomnia, and aggression.

Porphyrias
Another group of disorders that has been linked to a belief in vampires. Much less common than pellagra, porphyrias were traced to a gene mutation in the late-twentieth century. Sufferers developed characteristics befitting of vampires—with excessive exposure to sunlight often causing skin discoloration and blisters, thick hair on their faces and extremities, watery eyes, and neurological abnormalities.

Pricolici
In Romanian folklore, a werewolf in the form of a malicious (often yellow) dog that killed all regular dogs nearby—but one that could on occasion also transform into a bona fide wolf, a cat, or even a frog. Some people believed that pricolici were werewolves in life, returning as vampires after death.

Rabbi Judah Loew ben Bezalel
The best-known golem creator in Jewish folklore, Rabbi Loew (c. 1520–1609) lived in Prague. After studying the Kabbalah, he was said to have fashioned himself an artificial servant using mud from the bank of the Vltava river. The golem slept by day, and by night did everything its master commanded. One day it escaped, causing people to flee in fright. In a fit of rage, the golem then smashed everything in

its path before finally being chased away. See also **Golem** and **Homunculus.**

Radu

During the time of Vlad III's captivity (see **Matthias Corvinus**), the throne of Wallachia was occupied by his brother Radu, who reigned as an ally of the Hungarian king.

Renfield's Syndrome

Also known as "clinical vampirism," this is an obsession, usually among males, with drinking blood. Originating in the name of a character in Bram Stoker's novel *Dracula,* the term has been used widely, from psychiatry to popular culture, although it is not formally recognized it as a diagnostic condition; medical science has tended to include it as a subset of psychiatric disorders such as schizophrenia. Some say it stems from a blood-related experience in childhood that serves to link the idea of blood in affected individuals with sexual arousal. Various well-publicized murderers have been known to excel in vampiric rituals.

Saint Stephen I of Hungary

Saint Stephen (967 or 969 or 975–1038) was the first ruler of the Christian Kingdom of Hungary, crowned in the year 1000. Noted for discouraging pagan customs, he passed laws designed to protect the general public from a scourge of witches.

Satan
The evil adversary of God in modern Christian theology, often identified with the leader of the fallen angels and used as a synonym for "Devil." In the Hebrew Bible the name referred to various entities appointed by God to test humans' faith.

Sighişoara
This city in Transylvania—a region formerly ruled by Hungary but in Romania since 1918—is home to the fortress where Vlad III, the world's most famous alleged vampire, came unto this world and spent his formative years, though he later became ruler of Wallachia. His father, Vlad II, or Vlad Dracul ("Vlad the Dragon"; c. 1393–1447)—who had earlier been deposed from his Wallachian princely throne—was granted an estate here by Hungary's King Sigismund. Vlad III's house of birth stands here to this day. See also **Transylvania** and **Wallachia.**

Strigoi
Demonic creatures inhabiting Romanian folklore, these nocturnal death-birds—said to fly about at night, hunting human flesh and blood—were seen as troubled souls of the dead (or, sometimes, as living

people imbued with magical abilities). They could transform into other animals or become invisible. See also *Moroi* and *Vârcolac*.

The Strange Case of Dr. Jekyll and Mr. Hyde

In his 1886 novel, the Scottish novelist Robert Louis Stevenson (1850–1894) presented in Dr. Jekyll a well-respected London gentleman painfully aware that a darkness lurks within him. His solution fails miserably as he transforms into the embodiment of evil.

Transylvania

This historical region of western Romania, ruled for centuries by Hungary and bounded by the Carpathian mountains, has often been associated with vampires—in large part due to Bram Stoker's novel *Dracula*. While the historical figure most often linked with Dracula, Vlad III (aka Vlad the Impaler) was indeed born and raised here (see **Sighişoara**), he was in fact a ruler of Wallachia, the region to the south where he excelled in the tortures that earned him his nickname. See also **Wallachia**.

Vampire (Vampyre)

A mythological or folkloric being that feeds on the blood or a comparable, often spiritual life essence of the living. The term was popularized in the eighteenth century, though variants were such as the Romanian *strigoi* were also used. An older spelling, "Vampyre" has been adopted by many in the modern-day "Vampyre subculture" to differentiate themselves from those seen as wannabes.

Vampire bats
Goggle-eyed, blood-sucking bats belonging to the family of New World leaf-nosed bats. There is no evidence to suggest that they served as a basis for the creation of the vampire myths that spread through parts of medieval Europe.

Vampire Lifestyle
Linked with goth culture, this contemporary subculture derives from ideas regarding vampires found in contemporary fiction, although elements of sadomasochistic culture occasionally "bleeds" into it. Vampire lifestyle adherents comprise "sanguinarian vampires," who are known to actually drink each others' blood; and "psychic vampires," who take more abstract power from the life force of the living. Neither subset embraces the "emotional vampire" who is known to prey indiscriminately on one and all.

Vampire: The Masquerade
The first of White Wolf Publishing's World of Darkness role-playing games. For participants,

this represented a comprehensive new vampire mythology to live (or die) by. Blending elements of folklore, popular imagination, and religion in a self-professed "gothic-punk world," this game was to be succeeded by *Vampire: the Requiem* in 2004. The gloomy version of the real world that the Vampires inhabit is called the World of Darkness.

Vârcolac
The common term for "werewolf" in Romanian, although it can also refer to a "goblin." See also *Strigoi* and *Moroi*.

Vlad III (Vlad Țepeș, Vlad the Impaler)
The historical figure most associated with Count Dracula, Vlad III—Vlad Țepeș (the Impaler) as dubbed after his death—is linked in the popular imagination to Transylvania and to Hungarians despite the fact that he was a Vlach (Romanian) who ruled not in Transylvania, but in Wallachia. He was, however, born and raised in Transylvania. (See also **Sighișoara, Transylvania,** and **Wallachia.**) By all accounts an enthusiastic torturer, but probably for reasons other than being a vampire, he eventually fell in battle against the Ottoman Turks. His head was then cut off, preserved in honey, and sent to Sultan Mehmed II as a gift.

Voodoo (Vodou)

A religion whose roots go back to the Kingdom of Dahomey (present-day Behin) and other parts of West Africa. In Haiti (where it is spelled "vodou") and elsewhere in the Caribbean and Central American it flourished among African slaves and their descendants in a form blended with Christianity. Its primary spiritual force/creator is the god Bondyè, who remains hidden to mortals. Believers direct their worship of Bondyè through spirits called loa, whose favor they court via offerings, sacrifices, personal altars, devotional objects, and participation in ceremonies of music, dance, and spirit possession.

Wallachia

This region of present-day Romania, and not neighboring Transylvania (his birthplace and boyhood home), as imagined by many—was the *real* scene where the historical Dracula—Vlad III, who ruled over it in the second half of the fifteenth century—excelled in the tortures that posthumously earned him the moniker "the Impaler." See also **Sighişoara** and **Transylvania**.

Werewolf

In mythology and folklore, a person who could transform into a wolf or wolflike creature, whether inherently, after being cursed, or after being bitten by a werewolf. It was commonly held in Romanian villages for centuries that blood-sucking vampires could turn into wolves in a fit of rage.

Zombie

A soulless corpse believed to be animated by witchcraft and controlled by its creator/master for nefarious ends—especially in vodou as practiced in Haiti and elsewhere in the Caribbean. Zombies have deep roots in popular culture and folklore in North America and beyond. Modern-day research has determined that the "corpse" is in fact a living, albeit drugged human being. See also **Golem, Homunculus,** and **Voodoo.**

Bibliography

Balassa, Iván. *A határainkon túli magyarok néprajza*
(Hungarian Folklore Beyond Hungary's
Borders). Budapest: Gondolat, 1989.

Bíró, Ferencné, Csorba Csaba, and Rékassy Csaba.
Élet a középkori Európában és Magyarországon
(Life in Europe and Hungary During the
Middle Ages). Budapest: Móra Ferenc, 1985.

Bornemisza, Péter: *Ördögi kísértetekről* (On
Diabolical Ghosts). Budapest: Helikon, 1977.

Csőgör, Enikő. *Tordatúr hiedelemvilága* (The
Mythological World of Tordatúr [a village in
Transylvania]) Bucharest: Kriterion, 1998.

Dankanits, Ádám. XVI. *századi olvasmányok*
(Readings in the 16th Century). Bucharest:
Kriterion, 1974.

Dömötör, Tekla, ed. *Magyar néprajz – Népszokás-néphit, népi vallásosság* (Hungarian Folklore – Folk Customs, Beliefs, and Religious Practices). Budapest: Akadémiai, 1990.

Dömötör, Tekla. *A magyar nép hiedelemvilága* (The Mythological World of the Hungarian People). Budapest: Akadémiai, 1981.

Duby, Georges, and Robert Mandrou. *A francia civ ilizáció ezer éve* (A History of French Civilization). Budapest: Gondolat, 1975.

Durandin, Catherine. *A román nép története* (The History of the Romanians). Budapest: Maecenas, 1998.

Farkas, Jenő. *"A magyar Drakula"* (The Hungarian Dracula). Filmvilág (magazine), no. 12, 1997, Budapest.

Gautier, Théophile. *"Síron túli szerelem."* (Love Beyond the Grave) Galaktika (science fiction magazine), no. 51, 1983, Budapest.

Ortutay, Gyula, ed. *Magyar parasztmesék.*
(Hungarian Peasant Tales) Budapest:
Szépirodalmi, 1960.

Plion, Raymond. *"A vámpír."* (The Vampire)
Galaktika (science fiction magazine), no. 51,
1983, Budapest.

Ráth-Végh, István. *A varázsvessző* (The Magic
Wand). Budapest: Gondolat, 1979.

Stoker, Bram. *Drakula.* Westminster: Archibald
Constable and Company, 1897.

Strindberg, August. *Drámák – Haláltánc* (Plays –
The Dance of Death). Budapest: Európa, 1984.

Székely, György, ed. *Eszmetörténeti tanulmányok a
magyar középkorról.* (Studies in the History of
Ideas from the Hungarian Middle Ages).
Budapest: Akadémiai, 1984.

Tournier, Michel. *A vámpír röpte* (Le vol du
vampire). Budapest: Napvilág, 2006.

Index

ABOUT THE AUTHOR

István Pivárcsi is the author of twenty-two books in his native Hungary on a wide range of subjects, including short histories of witches and cannibalism, historical travelogues, and a history of political assassinations. His works are informed by his twenty-five years as a teacher of history at the college and high school levels, and his twenty years as a tour guide throughout Europe. *Just a Bite* was inspired by Pivárcsi's research into the customs, folklore, and mythology of various ethnic groups in and around Hungary—in particular, Transylvania, where he has spent many years leading tour groups on excursions to the very castles and villages connected with the historical figures behind such classic works as Bram Stoker's Dracula. He lives in Budapest.